Philip C. (Philip Christopher) Friese

Semitic Philosophy

Showing the ultimate social and scientific Outcome of original Christianity in its

Conflict with surviving Ancient Heathenism

Philip C. (Philip Christopher) Friese

Semitic Philosophy
Showing the ultimate social and scientific Outcome of original Christianity in its Conflict with surviving Ancient Heathenism

ISBN/EAN: 9783337071646

Printed in Europe, USA, Canada, Australia, Japan

Cover: Foto ©ninafisch / pixelio.de

More available books at **www.hansebooks.com**

SEMITIC PHILOSOPHY:

SHOWING

THE ULTIMATE SOCIAL AND SCIENTIFIC OUTCOME

OF ORIGINAL CHRISTIANITY

IN ITS CONFLICT WITH

SURVIVING ANCIENT HEATHENISM.

BY

PHILIP C. FRIESE.

CHICAGO:

S. C. GRIGGS & COMPANY,

1890.

CONTENTS.

CHAPTER I.

CHAPTER II.

MAN'S ORIGINAL PHILOSOPHY, or First Thought,
WHEN IN CONSCIOUS RELATION TO OTHER SPIRITS, FIRST,
WITHOUT LANGUAGE, IN NATURAL SOCIETY, THEN WITH
LANGUAGE, IN ARTIFICIAL SOCIETY, WAS AT FIRST IN
BOTH CASES NORMAL; UNTIL ANCIENT ARTIFICIAL SOCIETY,
BY THE LAPSE OF MAN'S THOUGHT THROUGH THE ABUSE
OF LANGUAGE INTO IDOLATRY AND BY THE REDUCTION
OF HIS PRACTICAL ACTION THROUGH IDOLATRY INTO CRIME,
BECAME, AS THE UNION OF IDOLATRY AND CRIME, AB-
NORMAL, AND WAS CALLED ANCIENT HEATHENISM, . 35–64

CHAPTER III.

THE DOCTRINE AND THE PRACTICE OF THE KINGDOM OF GOD, BEING THE REVIVAL BY JESUS OF NORMAL ARTIFICIAL SOCIETY FROM ANCIENT HEATHENISM BY MEANS OF THE REVIVAL OF THE SPECULATIVE SIDE, AND THE CONSEQUENT REVIVAL OF THE PRACTICAL SIDE OF THE ORIGINAL OR SEMITIC PHILOSOPHY, . 65-98

CHAPTER IV.

CHAPTER V.

CHAPTER VI.

INTRODUCTION.

THE Semitic Philosophy is the doctrine of the Kingdom of God, as it was first, under circumstances of very great difficulty, briefly proclaimed, and as it is capable of unlimited development. It is a system of principles, of first truths, based on patent facts of the universe, and couched in a brief formula.

The fact that its author did not write it down in a book, suggests that he did not regard it as altogether beholden, for its preservation or for its development, to elaborate written forms of human language, or to any rigid verbal methods. The inference, indeed, is clear, that he relied, for the extension and propagation of his doctrine, on something entirely different from words.

That there is, and always has been, another, though always much neglected, vehicle of thought, an internal instrument, altogether diverse from spoken or written words, is for every person that reflects a moment upon the process that, when he thinks, takes place within him, a most palpable truth. When he thinks of an object, or group of objects, not present, he sees within him something that represents it; and which, when the object is a physical one, that he has before observed, and when its representation is vivid, he clearly perceives not to be either a word or a group of words, but an apparently distinct image of it, which, if he were not aware that the object was not present, he could not distinguish from the object itself. Now, the thing that vividly represents in thought an absent object, and that seems its image, may be called its sensuous idea.

The nature of the sensuous ideas and their uses deserve attention. They can be proved to be material; to be organic parts of man's body, located, probably, in the brain; constructed like the rest of the body, by man's spirit; and marked with significant signs by forces rayed upon them, through the senses, from outward objects. It is they that immediately represent to man's spirit, outward objects, whether absent or present. Even words, oral or written, as outward ideas or representations of objects, are represented by the inward sensuous ideas, before they can be known.

The thought carried on by means of sensuous ideas, without words, is instinctive. Sometimes, it is so rapid that its separate steps cannot be remembered, but only its result; and its process is virtually unconscious. At other times its steps are deliberate and perfectly conscious. The advantage of instinctive thought, on account of its vividness and rapidity, over thought conducted by means of words, is manifested by its almost exclusive use in the common affairs of daily life. Its superiority is equally obvious in the constructions of the highest science, by means of the sensuous ideas resulting from careful observations and experiments.

Without impugning the proper advantages of language for recording and communicating truth, the appropriate adaptation of instinctive thought for investigating, exploring, methodizing, building up, and developing an embryonic system of social doctrine, as was that of the Kingdom of God when first proclaimed, embracing by implication all liberal culture, and including philosophy, the special sciences, and the practical disciplines of religion, industry, charity and government, is unquestionable.

Committed to the keeping of mere language, the doctrine of the Kingdom of God would have come down to us as a dogmatic, illiberal, contracted, dwarfed, and stunted abortion. But faithfully and generously confided, as the "comforter" of mankind, to the instinctive thought of the learned and the unlearned alike, it has been not only preserved, but cherished and developed, by the study of learned scholars, and by the tradition of the unlearned masses of the people; until it has grown from the tenets of a small and despised sect, to become the rule and the ideal, not only of modern civilization, but, also, of that more perfect universal, Interrace society which modern civilization, by proving the increasing capacity of the masses of the people for liberal culture, clearly foreshadows.

Combinations of true sensuous ideas revealed in sudden glory, like constellations and galaxies of distant

stars, shining forth in the night, and skilfully suggested by Jesus, represented truths to the spirit of
man which could not in his time be fully interpreted by
the heathen words then current, and as then understood. For the languages known to the circle in
which Jesus personally moved were imperfect and
undeveloped; and in that circle little cultivation of
those languages prevailed. It would have been necessary to invent a body of new technical terms, that is a
new and extremely difficult language beyond the easy
comprehension of the common people, to express at
large and in an intelligible way the newly proclaimed
truth of the Kingdom of God.

Since that time new meaning has been infused into
modern language, which has become reconstructed in
new tongues and dialects, and has now in its various
modifications, in Christian nations, become a better
vehicle of Christian thought.

But, if Jesus had attempted to write his doctrine
in any of the imperfect languages of his day, it would
have been necessarily liable to gross misinterpretation.
By not writing his doctrine, he has referred its keeping to the sensuous ideas, where it always was, and
where, in its original purity and truth, it always will
be, found by earnest searchers with the instruments of
deliberate instinctive thought.

Many of the so-called religious dogmas of the day
are linguistic formulations, couched in language that
preserves its heathen implications, and which, therefore,

fails to fully express them in a Christian sense; although they were first suggested, perhaps, by deep, far away, indistinctly perceived truth.

By treating in the light of instinctive thought, and by means of the sensuous ideas, what we have called the Semitic philosophy as the doctrine of the Kingdom of God, this philosophy can be carried back, before the origin of language, and, therefore, independently of it, to the primeval man, as well as carried forward to that ultimate consummation of perfect universal society, which is the ideal goal of all reform, and in which all merely human language must give place to other purely spiritual modes of intercourse.

The lifegiving, energizing, and developing influence of instinctive, or free, thought upon the inward growth and the outward extension of the doctrine of the Kingdom of God, can then be contrasted with the deadening obstruction fastened upon its vital functions by the cumbrous load of merely verbal, and arbitrary symbols, creeds, dogmas, canons, and decrees, that in some quarters have hindered, and in others have totally stopped its progress, and have turned it backwards towards the errors of ancient heathenism.

No form of words can fully express, although it may indicate, a principle, far less a system or doctrine of principles. A principle can only be reached, by means of the sensuous ideas, in free or instinctive thought. Words, like a boat, may conduct us to the continent of truth; but, if we would explore the continent, we must leave the boat behind us, and follow whither our inward guides, the faithful, unerring sensuous ideas, lead.   We only go back to our boat when we wish to report our discoveries to those we left behind.

P. C. F.

BALTIMORE, January 4, 1890.

CHAPTER I.

THE Semitic Philosophy, so called from the race of the author of its great revival, is the Christian doctrine of the Kingdom of God. It was man's first thought, as an isolated person, before the invention of language, and being conducted by means of the sensuous ideas before its revival, it was the instinctive and normal original philosophy.

1. To avoid any misconception from the name of the Semitic Philosophy, and from its relation to the doctrine of the Kingdom of God, it seems necessary to make two preliminary remarks. In the first place, it should be said that the Semitic Philosophy, like the doctrine of the Kingdom of God, with which, in its developed sense, it is virtually synonymous, does not propose to enounce the principles of the science of religion only, but of all the sciences, and especially of all social science; deriving all principles from its one universal First Principle. In the second place, it is proper to say, that the Semitic Philosophy, while based on instinctive, or free, thought, and departing from some of the verbiage of prevailing systems, and particularly eschewing the trammels of obsolete, ancient, and arbitrary verbal maxims, creeds and dogmas, does not, in putting forth its views with the perfect freedom that belongs to truth, "come to destroy the law;" but "to

fulfil" in every jot and tittle the Higher Law of God; for with this law must all true philosophy agree.

There are many interesting and important systems of philosophy. They all propose, in avoiding the details of the special sciences, while having a tacit reference to them all, to give general views and explanations respecting the nature of man, and both of the material universe, and of the society, in which he is placed. Those systems which recognize God and his true relations to man, include in this society, expressly or by implication, the superior and presiding spirit of the one God.

These systems have been composed at different and widely separated periods; some being very ancient, and others quite modern. All have much in common; but while each gives a condensed epitome of the highest culture of the times in which its author wrote, or verbally expounded his doctrine, they are said, upon the whole, in combining ancient wisdom with modern improvements, to exhibit a decided progress.

A new system of philosophy, therefore, cannot now be made entirely new, without culpably disregarding the merits of the old. But, if it eliminates from the systems that have preceded it some important error, or adds to these systems some hitherto neglected weighty truths, it may in these respects, without presumptuously contending for the glory of a brilliant creation of genius, make a modest claim to attention on the ground of novelty. It is also possible, as will now be attempted, by disregarding the verbiage of prevailing systems, to ascend, by instinctive thought, to the simple philosophy of primeval man.

Philosophy has been called the science of sciences, the science of knowledge, the science of being, the science of principles, the science of the universal, the study of the cosmos; and, in fact, it is all of these. For it is an integral discipline, and each of its functions involves in its exercise all the rest; while each of these definitions merely brings one of its functions into prominence.

Viewed as a seeking after the universal, it begins in childhood; for the child is ever making wider and wider classes of the things surrounding it, and higher and higher generalizations; investigating with curiosity the part of the universe within its reach, and seeking to comprehend its significance, and to utilize it for realizing its practical schemes.

Indeed, the system of the kindergarten, as a method of primary education, is profoundly philosophical in recognizing and developing the surprising fund of thought without language, or the instinctive thought, exhibited by the young child before it has learned the language to express it; yet which is strictly carried on, as will be explained, by means of the sensuous ideas; and which, if expressed in learned language, would well deserve the name of philosophy. For the instinctive thought of the child is constantly reaching after the universal.

A lower, but still a remarkable, degree of reasoning, without language, is shown by many wild and domestic animals, and by insects, which exhibit instinctive thought in traces of foresight, prudence, mechanical skill, and industrial combination, in their work.

But not only in children and animals does instinctive thought take place in the absence of language. It is a remarkable fact that the greater part of the reasoning performed by all grown men, learned and unlearned alike, perhaps ninety-nine hundredths of it, is carried on instinctively, without the use of language. This fact, on reflection, is as evident as it is important; plainly disclosing philosophy at work in a new and unexpected field.

2. Indeed, it cannot be doubted, that a large portion of the instinctive thought, as well of the unlearned masses as of the learned few, is true philosophy, or general reasoning based upon the highest universal principles. Many instances can be given in which a universal principle announced by some scholar from his study, or by some man of business to his associates, has been taken up by those that heard it, and spread over a nation, over a continent, and over the whole civilized world—with some help, indeed, of language and of the press, as well as with some opposition from them—but with a speed that no such help can explain. For although the spoken word and the press can circulate the statement or formula of a principle far and wide, with some of the reasoning calculated to enforce its acceptance, experience proves that at first they will find only "a paucity" of hearers and read-. ers. A striking formula in which the principle is expressed may be remembered; but it is the afterthought, the instinctive free thought, of the people in silence, in solitude, or at their work, that collects from far and near and applies those arguments and motives from every source, that support the principle and make it a guiding and controlling popular force.

For instance, a distinguished lawyer once asserted that

there is "a higher law than the Constitution." The expression, bearing on the questions and discussions that were agitating the people, attracted attention, and seemed almost immediately to command conviction and the support of millions. But before the principle involved could be rationally accepted, there was required a comparatively long train of reasoning—of reasoning opposed to the hereditary sentiments and maxims of the people, coming down from past generations, and urged by trusted and patriotic men of gigantic intellect—as Daniel Webster, who had gained immortal glory by defending the Constitution against another line of attack. The reasoning of the people in their afterthought on this subject was necessarily, in most cases, instinctive.

The principle claimed to be the higher law, was the right of personal liberty, which was instinctively or intuitively seen to be a law of nature, and as such to be a law of God, and was therefore concluded to be paramount over the Constitution, which is positive law, and as such is made by man—a conclusion intuitively and instinctively reached in opposition to the tons of legal reports and legal text-books yearly scattered over the country, to the great mass of the current literature, and probably to the majority of sermons at that time preached. The instinctive nature of the reasoning which impelled the movement of the people in favor of the higher law, will be most clearly apprehended, as well as its force, from the rapidity and universality of its action.

If this movement is traced from its defensive position in the comparatively small body of its early adherents, the Abolition party, when they united with their fellow citizens, who had then no sympathy with this movement, in the Northern, the Western and the Border states, to resist the actual revolution and civil war that chiefly aimed to dissolve the union of the United States and to seize a part of its territory, it will be evident that, in the midst of this revolution and civil war, a sudden counter revolution against slavery, and in favor of the higher law, and inaugurated by the Proclamation of Emancipation, swept over the whole country.

This counter revolution changed the issues of the war. The General Government reluctantly adopted the views of the Abolitionists as a war measure. For it was evident, that if slavery could be abolished, there would be no longer any motive for dissolving the Union, or for dividing the common country of the States. Both sides acknowledged that the new issue of the abolition of slavery, in accordance with the higher law, took precedence over the first issues of the war, and must be settled first.

Battles were fought after the new issue was made up; but the decisive battle, the real tug of war, was on the field of reason. The instinctive thought of the people was set to work, and through its electric action the dark cloud of slavery disappeared from the political horizon, and left " not a rack behind."

The force of the instinctive thought of the people was demonstrated by the fact that the whole people, the masses as well as the highly educated classes, in the South and in the North, came at once to the same conclusion, and acquiesced in it without reserve; namely, that slavery, notwithstanding all the positive laws and judicial decisions made in favor of it, was illegal as well as immoral, being a violation of the paramount higher law; and that, as it could not be justified, it could not be defended.

If it be said that the rapid spread and the ultimate success of the principle of the higher law was due to military force, and to the victory of the supporters of that doctrine on the field of battle, the answer is that force, although it may put down outward opposition and compel outward conformity, cannot produce conviction. The practice of slavery was doubtless, in a great measure, suppressed by military force; but the sincere abandonment of the doctrine of slavery, and the adoption of the higher law, could not be effected by force, and must have been caused by reasoning; and that reasoning, spreading in so short a time its legitimate logical conclusion from a few Abolitionists to the general body of the people, must have been instinctive.

3. Similarly, there have been other revolutions,— the French Revolution, the American Revolution, the English Revolution; and before these, the religious revolutions called the conversions of the Saxons, Prussians, Russians and some other European nations to Christianity, and the revolutionary spread of Mohammedanism, in all of which movements force was used to overthrow and suppress ancient practices;—while the ultimate, peaceful and virtually unanimous conformity of the masses of the people to the new doctrines can only be explained as the result of instinctive reasoning. So in the Middle Ages, by the same reasoning, and not by learned discussions and treatises, was established in the

masses the principle of the separate organization of industry, leading to the erection of free cities and to the limitation of the monarchical governments of Europe, by means of organized trade guilds.

But instinctive thought is interesting, not only for what it has accomplished in the past, but also for what it is able and will be called on, to do in the future. There are impending movements, peaceful revolutions, practical social reforms,—both in primary and in liberal public education, in the general Church, in the organization of industry, in the system of public charity, and in the simplification and organization of the various branches of government,—which must be first fully thought out, and then worked out, by the masses of the people; and which are so vast in their scope, and so multitudinous in their details, that they can only be fully thought out instinctively.

Formal dogmatic methods would be far too narrow, and far too slow. But, when the fundamental principle of each needed social reform is once clearly stated,— then, with whatever aid the common fund of language can afford for consultation and comparison of views, and with occasional light from some learned thinker,—the masses of the people will be responsible for carrying the principle out to its full practical realization in a general advance of modern civilization, under the guidance of instinctive reasoning.

4. It is highly important, therefore, to examine the nature of instinctive thought, and for this purpose to consider the means it employs. These may be called the sensuous ideas.

They enable man, without language, to discover the first of all principles, and under its guidance to carry on instinctively the most important and complicated train of reasoning. Their examination will lead us up to that first principle, from which all the derivative principles of speculative and of practical action can be deduced; and which is the basis of that first covenant of God with man, which is the original and continuing social contract, the fundamental unwritten constitution of society:—the principle, therefore, that must underlie all philosophy.

That which will appear to be most novel in the system of philosophy now proposed, will be that it pays more attention than other systems to the instinctive action of man, both practical and in thought.

5. There is, in fact, but one philosophy. It is a perfect, unwritten; instinctive, predominantly speculative ideal. It is the Knowledge of God,—involving all truth and goodness, and written, as the prophet says, on man's heart. It rests on the first implied covenant of God with man, the promised uniformity of the uniformities of God's action, or of the laws of nature;—that uniformity which is the highest law of the kingdom of God, and is the basis of Christianity, of modern civilization;—the first principle of all science and of all practice.

Many systems of philosophy, and, to represent their peculiar doctrines, respectively, many so-called fundamental questions, have been proposed. But all the fundamental questions of true philosophy form one universal, integral, or organic question. The universal and at the same time integral or organic question of all philosophy is: How is man related to the Kingdom of God, as the rational system of the universe? It involves the problem of rationally conducting man's normal, speculative and practical life, whether instinctive or fully conscious, under the conditions presented by the actual universe.

The formula, Kingdom of God, implies, and it has always been regarded as implying a philosophy, which may be expanded into a compact, consistent statement of the highest principles or laws of the spiritual and material universe, as its fundamental regulative constitution; this being the sum of the laws of nature or of God; all of which may be grasped into the one first principle as the uniformity of the uniformities of God's action. Hence, this formula necessarily implies, on the one hand, a rational, organic, or integral system of thought; which explains, on the other hand, the universe as a rational organism of being, including society as an organic association, under the social contract of all men with God.

The philosophy of the formula, Kingdom of God, may be called the Semitic Christian philosophy, in distinction from the ancient philosophies of Greece and Rome and of the Orient, and from the modern outgrowths of those antiquated roots. It is instinctive as well as implied, and is, therefore, unwritten, being thereby distinguished from all other systems of philosophy. All its principles were proclaimed in the one first principle implied in the formula, Kingdom of God; and were then preserved by popular tradition in the language of the common sense and public opinion of modern civilization; and were also constantly confirmed, independently of language, by the mechanism of unspoken instinctive thought, used, as will be explained, by the learned and the unlearned alike.

It must, as all philosophy, be a theory both of knowledge and of practice, as well as an inquiry into the nature of things. We must enter upon philosophy by the way of thought, and then through thought we shall learn something of being.

Thought and being are intimately connected as cause and effect; and hence they cannot be identical. We know being as the predominant cause of our thought, and our thought as the predominant effect of being on our spirit.

We begin to philosophize by investigating the process of conscious thought, because the process of instinctive thought is in general partly unconscious; and it cannot, therefore, be fully inspected at the very time when it takes place; but, like all unconscious action, it can be proved afterwards by circumstantial evidence.

In the first place, man's conscious thought performed without language, will be examined in man, both as an isolated individual, and in primitive or natural society, as the associate of God and of his fellow-men, whom that thought makes known to him. Afterwards, the use of language, and the danger of its abuse, in his thought, will be shown.

In fact, before language there was thought. For language is proved, by the vast variety of the languages always found in the world, to be the invention of man ; and thought was evidently necessary to suggest, guide, and develop man's action in the formation of language. The greater part of the thought that prevailed before language, was necessarily instinctive; and it is the unquestionable fact, that instinctive thought, owing to its superior speed and certainty, has remained, after the invention of language, the larger portion of the thought which both the learned and the unlearned now carry on. It will be seen, on investigation, that the same means or instruments that are employed in instinctive thought, are also used in all the conscious thought performed without language.

Thought, with its connected practical action, will be examined (I.) in the isolated individual without language; (II.) in man connected with other living beings, plant or animal, human or divine, without language, in natural society; and (III.) in artificial society, with language.

6. I. The investigation of conscious thought in the assumed isolated individual without language, who may represent the primeval man, may be considered as beginning either at the first dawn of consciousness in the life of infancy, or on the awaking of the individual in mature life from sleep. The first steps of the investigation, in both cases, must be virtually the same; the only difference being that in infancy they succeed each other much more slowly.

7. In both cases consciousness is preceded by a state of unconsciousness more or less complete; and this state of unconsciousness is proved, in both cases, by circumstantial evidence, that will be mentioned hereafter, to have been one of extremely varied, perfectly accurate, practical instinctive action.

The awaking of consciousness from unconsciousness, is the concrete beginning of a section of subsequent concrete conscious life; and every such beginning necessarily involves every other beginning that has preceded it, and consequently also its absolute beginning, to the conception of which it is the nearest approach that can be made. For it is self-evident that we cannot conceive either the absolute beginning or the absolute ending of anything.

But every concrete beginning is also a concrete ending of what went before; and so a concrete ending is a concrete beginning of something following, not altogether new. Thus there is an alternation, indefinitely repeated, of man's conscious with his unconscious life, producing a probable immortality, that may be compared to the conservation of energy, in its alternating forms, in the outward world. Solomon said, "There is nothing new under the sun"—in the sense of absolutely new;—as every effect must have been involved in its cause. We may extend his remark, if he did not, to regions beyond the earth. For the concrete endings of conscious life on earth must, as causes, result in effects as concrete beginnings, if not on the earth, then in the same universe beyond it.

Commencing, now, our investigation at the beginning of man's concrete consciousness, and passing by minor details that belong to psychology, the first step of philosophy is the conservative analysis of awaking consciousness, displaying for our observation its separate parts, while preserving their normal relations and their organic connections.

The difference between a conservative and a destructive analysis of an animal organization, is like that between

vivisection and butchering. Similarly, in all integral or
organic wholes, or things composed of integral or ideal
parts, each part pervading the whole and the whole each
part; as in spiritual organisms, or in the action of spirit,
or of the reason, or of the mind;—while a conservative
analysis preserves, in the interaction and articulation of
the integral or ideal parts, the integrity and the common
life of the whole, a destructive analysis deprives them all
of healthy life, by attempting to sever the integral or ideal
parts from their natural articulations with each other,
as if they were independent and irrespective organs or
faculties, and by thus taking away the aid which each, in
performing its appropriate action, derives from the others.

It is a common, if not a universal error, to apply a
destructive analysis to the action of man's spirit, or of
the mind. Its reason, understanding, sense, judgment,
imagination, memory, will, are cut off and disconnected
from each other; and these dissevered members are made
to go through spasmodic actions, like the galvanized
limbs carved off from the body of a dead animal. But,
as no complete life, either of any spiritual or of any animal organism, can take place without the perfect union
and co-operation of all its organic parts, a conservative
analysis of it, instead of sundering, will carefully preserve
intact, and exhibit in full view, all the connections of its
parts and their means of reciprocal interaction.

The first operation made by such a conservative
analysis upon man's awaking consciousness, is to distinguish from each other its two main elements, the active
subject, or the self, or the spirit of man, and the present
inert object of the subject's action.

Continuing the conservative analysis of consciousness, and omitting for the present unnecessary psychological details, we will find that this analysis must pursue a different course in regard to each of the two elements into which consciousness is divided.

The first of these elements, the subject, or man's spirit, is an indivisible spiritual unit, the distinguishing attribute of which is its life, or action; and it is to its action, as an integral whole, with integral parts, that the analysis must be applied.

The other element of consciousness is man's body, an organic material instrument, the distinguishing attribute of which is its passivity and its inertness; so that its conservative analysis must distinguish the adaptation of its several articulated organic parts to subserve the various modes of the spirit's action.

The body is called material or matter to distinguish it from the spirit; because in their qualities, as has been well observed, they are altogether different from each other, and have no attribute in common. The term spirit will be used instead of the terms subject, mind, or soul, or interchangeably with them, when any one of them is employed to express an indivisible spiritual unit, in direct contrast to a material body.

The analysis of the body will be naturally preceded by that of the spirit's action, to which the body as its instrument is subservient. For the first conscious relation of the spirit to the body, as manifested in conscious action, is that of the agent to its instrument. Another relation between them, originating in the spirit's unconscious life preceding consciousness, will be mentioned hereafter.

8. In the conservative analysis of the action of man's spirit, to which we now proceed, the first division of this action is into its two fundamental elements of speculative or cognitive, and practical action; then each of these may be immediate or mediate; or, again, unconscious or conscious; or, further, real or imaginative. As the action or life of man's spirit is an integral whole, the parts resulting from its conservative analysis must likewise be integral — each pervading the whole, and each interpenetrated by the rest. Every cognitive or speculative act of the spirit, whether immediate or mediate, unconscious or conscious, real or imaginative,— is aided by some or all of its modes of practical action; and every practical act of the spirit is guided by one or more of its speculative modes.

But, while all the elements of the spirit's action, and all their subordinate modes must co-operate in every act, one of its fundamental elements, in one of its various modes, must in every act predominate. Predominately speculative action, therefore, though called simply speculative, is partly practical; and predominately practical action is always partly speculative.

The qualities of normal and abnormal, or of good and evil, do not belong to the action of the isolated individual; and they will only come to be noticed when man is considered in society.

Owing to the integral nature of the spirit's action, the unconscious mode of its action must sometimes, to some extent, be simultaneous with, and sometimes almost entirely pass into, its conscious mode. Hence, the term instinctive action will be sometimes used in place of the term unconscious action,—it being understood that the instinctive action of the spirit is predominately unconscious, although it often tends to become, and at times partly, and at other times altogether, does become, conscious.

The instinctive action of the spirit, whether speculative or practical, is not observed at the time it takes place, because it is for the most part unconscious; but, when it is practical, it is afterwards proved, by competent conscious circumstantial evidence, to have occurred; and when it is speculative, its results indicate the reasoning that led to them. The circumstantial evidence to prove foregone practical instinctive action, is the effects or changes, of which it must have been the cause.

The first conscious speculative action of the spirit, after distinguishing the subject from the object, is its intuition of the facts constituting, as effects, the circumstantial evidence of its preceding unconscious or instinctive practical action. These effects are its body.

9. Man's body is notoriously composed of the material elements surrounding it, and which he consciously, by eating and drinking, and unconsciously, by breathing, places within it, and thereby in immediate relation to his spirit. When he moves his body, which he knows to be an object, and different in every respect from his spirit, and therefore to be matter, he is conscious that its motion is caused by the immediate practical action of his spirit; and, as soon as he learns that there are other spirits besides himself, he infers, by analogy, that every original motion of matter is caused by the immediate practical action of some spirit. Hence, as by every conscious or

instinctive movement of his body man demonstrates that within it his spirit, by its instinctive, immediate, practical action, can move, and therefore use, matter, he infers that his spirit, which he thus knows to be a sufficient and present agent, does in fact use the matter within his body for building it up and repairing it.

If it can be shown that the sensuous ideas within man, representing outward things to man's spirit, are material, and are organic parts of man's body, it will also follow that they, too, are made by the spirit's instinctive, immediate, practical action.

It may be observed, in passing, that the ideas here mentioned, and afterwards described, are virtually the same things understood, by the same term, by Plato, Aristotle, Kant, Locke, Hume, Berkeley, Descartes, and others; all of whom, while differing from each other as to the nature and proper use of the ideas, saw them as plainly and used them as habitually, as they saw and used the sun. But no philosopher seems to have been always consistent in his views concerning them. Plato was perhaps the most inconsistent. For, besides giving his well known fanciful and utterly absurd philosophical explanation of the ideas — an explanation confuted at the time by Aristotle — he has left for universal admiration a poetic figure, which foreshadows, although it only dimly foreshadows, the true representative nature of the sensuous ideas. He describes a cave, and a man within it, facing its back, and watching the shadows flitting there and cast through its mouth, which is behind him, by passing persons and things of the outward world. But we shall see that the sensuous ideas are more than flitting shadows; that a pencil of light from without photographs upon them in the brain the shifting scenes, and writes upon the heart the universal laws, of the outward universe; and that man's spirit within his body, like Plato's watcher in his cave, looks not outward for knowledge of the outer world, but scans its faithful messages imprinted on living tablets within him.

That the representative sensuous ideas are material, is a self-evident fact. For they are objects, intuitively seen, and known, by the spirit's immediate speculative action, to possess the primary qualities of matter, especially magnitude; and also color, motion, and relative place. That they are organic parts of the body, follows from the facts that they are within the body, and are, so far as is known, inseparable from it, at least for definite periods of time, and certainly contribute, with the rest of the body, to give the spirit, in all its speculative and practical functions, most important aid. Hence, as parts of the body, they must be made, with the rest of it, by the spirit's immediate practical action.

The conservative analysis of man's body, the creature, as we have seen, as well as the instrument, of his spirit, will exhibit it as an organism, or a collective instrument composed of many co-operating parts or organs, and perfectly adapted to serve and facilitate both the speculative and the practical action, unconscious as well as conscious, of man's spirit.

For the explanation of all the modes of the spirit's action, a specification of all the organs or integral parts of its collective instrument, the body, would be necessary. But all those organs, chiefly internal, that minister

to the part of life that is common to man and the
lower animals, may be left to physiology. For we are
only concerned now with man's higher life as a rational
being, and with those of his bodily organs that directly
serve it. Of these bodily organs it is only necessary to
mention here the outward bodily frame and its outward
members, with the five outward senses, and the inward
appendages of the latter, the brain and sensuous ideas.

10. Among these bodily organs it is only the sensuous
ideas that call for any extended remarks. The outward
frame of the body, its outward members, and its outward
senses, are sufficiently known to contribute both to the
speculative and the practical action of the spirit; and the
brain has been proved by specialists to be connected,
through the nerves, with the outward senses; and to be
the seat of important action communicated through
them from the outward world. The particulars concerning the uses of these parts of the body need not detain us.

The sensuous ideas having been shown to be intimately connected with the spirit's unconscious, or, as we
shall now call it, instinctive action, as effects which that
action practically causes, they will now be exhibited as
the means which it speculatively employs. The use of
the sensuous ideas to represent outward things, will be
explained, somewhat at large, to be independent of
language.

11. Besides the representative sensuous ideas described
above, and easily proved, like them, to be material, by
exhibiting the primary qualities of matter, the spirit,
by its combined speculative and practical action, frames
and introduces among them what are known as the

imaginative or fictitious ideas; evidently composed of the
same kind of highly plastic matter as the representative
ideas, but marked and modeled by the spirit, to serve
either as mementos of some broad generalizations or
lofty abstractions; or as ideals, schemes, plans, and pro-
jects for future realization and execution.

The imaginative or fictitious ideas obviously answer,
as is well known, a very valuable end both in science and
in the fine and useful arts, so that little more need be
now said concerning them. It is evident that they do
not make their appearance in consciousness until long
after the representative sensuous ideas.

In the conservative analysis of awaking consciousness,
to which we now return, we have advanced to the consideration of the representative and the imaginative sensuous ideas, viewed as organic parts of the body, and as
constructed by the spirit's instinctive, immediate, practical action. Being within the body, and therefore in
the immediate presence of the spirit, its immediate speculative action, or intuition, is exerted upon them. This,
according to its rapidity, is either instinctive and partly
unconscious, or fully and deliberately conscious. Instinctive speculative action, as we shall presently see, is
so very rapid that but few of its steps can be remembered. Its results are conscious and are highly important; but the instinctive process, by which they are
reached, can only be apprehended and described in
general, and without detailing its separate stages.
We are first concerned to know what the spirit, in its
intuitive conscious thought, observes in the sensuous
ideas; and what use, in its several modes of speculative

and practical action, it makes of them, without language, and as an isolated individual.

12. It seems proper, however, before describing what the spirit of man observes in the sensuous ideas, and before stating, in general, the use that it makes of them, without language, in its speculative and practical action, as an isolated individual, to enumerate the various modifications, of speculative and practical action; and to observe that in all these modifications, except for the purpose of communicating thought, the use of the sensuous ideas without language will suffice. In this way, the true value of language will be noticed and enhanced, by recognizing that its proper sphere of usefulness is to communicate, record, disseminate, and preserve thought; thereby making the use of thought joint, and thus promoting associations for joint practical action; while all the processes of individual or original thought, and of individual practical action, can be carried on without language, by means of sensuous ideas alone.

Now, while the spirit's speculative action, as a whole, is designated as mind, or intellect, or understanding, or speculative reason, the chief modifications of its individual, or original speculative action, are called sensation, sense, intuition, presentation, representation, knowing, thinking, judgment, comparison, classification, generalization, notion, concept, inference, induction, deduction, imagination, memory, and speculative faith; and while the spirit's practical action, as a whole, is called the practical reason, the chief modifications of its original or individual practical action, are named will, desire, intention, purpose, planning, scheming, expectation, hope, passion, anger, and practical faith. It must always, however, be borne in mind, that, owing to the integral nature of the spirit's action, every exercise of its speculative mode of action is combined with some mode of its practical action, and every exercise of its practical action, with some mode of its speculative action. But, in presenting a general view of the spirit's speculative and practical action, as an integral whole, it is not necessary to enter upon a strict discrimination of the multitude of terms used to express its parts.

13. It should also be observed here, that feeling, or emotion, although a highly important incident of action, is not a distinct and independent mode of action, between the speculative and the practical modes; but is a mark or attribute, pleasurable or painful, belonging to various modes of practical and speculative action, serving as an instinctive æsthetic guide for their exercise, though always subordinate to the reason, and to faith. For although instinct is undeveloped reason, it shows its inferiority when it conflicts with reason, which is fully developed instinct, and still more when it conflicts with faith, which is fully developed reason. The main cause of the importance of feeling,—as we shall see when we pass from the action of the isolated individual to the action of society,—is the fact that the same feeling, in a modified degree, results from fictitious or imaginative action as from real action, and from fictitious or imaginative ideas, as from real representative sensuous ideas. For this fact is the basis of all the fine arts.

14. We are now prepared to describe what the spirit observes in the representative sensuous ideas, and to

explain what use, independent of language, it makes of
them in thought: They are commonly called images of
outward things, but this is a figurative expression.
All that the spirit actually sees in the sensuous ideas,
overlooking in respect to them as well as the other
inward parts of the body the fact that they are matter,
are certain marks, impressions, and signs inscribed upon
each of them, and altogether, or nearly altogether, different upon each.

Only a brief experience is necessary to satisfy the
spirit that the inscriptions it observes upon the sensuous ideas are significant. As a ship is built with a form
adapted to traverse the uneven surface of the sea, to ride
and breast its rolling waves, so man's body is constructed with a form suited to travel over the rough
surface of the land, and to navigate over it, amidst a
throng of fixed and moving solid objects. Thus, the
form of the body points to the existence of an outward
world beyond it; and accordingly when the body successively approaches different outward objects, comes in contact with them, or departs from them, and when the
spirit observes corresponding changes in the marks upon
its sensuous ideas, it associates these changes with
related facts in the outward world. Soon, certain marks
upon these ideas are associated with the near presence of
certain outward objects. Then, some of these outward
objects are further identified, as those actually present,
by the senses of touch, of smell, of taste, and of hearing,
giving corroborating supplementary marks, when the
primary or prominent marks proceed from the sense of

sight; and by the sense of sight, when the primary or prominent marks proceed from the other senses.

The marks upon the sensuous ideas may be explained as impressions made upon them by forces rayed or reflected upon them, in lines or undulations, through the several outward senses, from outward objects. Among such forces, are light, heat, electricity.

The representative sensuous ideas, with their marks, may be further regarded not only as loosely indicating the presence of their respective outward objects, but also as exact differentials of them, or as indefinitely small auxiliary magnitudes, precisely representing them all on the same scale; and thus giving to the process both of conscious and of instinctive thought the certainty and combining power of mathematics. Indeed, the differential and integral calculus of the mathematics may be looked upon simply as an instance of success in imitating, by momentarily arresting, correctly observing, and carefully educing into consciousness, and then into verbal and symbolic expression, the fleeting and rapid but certain method of instinctive thought.

But, while the differentials of mathematics are all primarily quantitative, the sensuous ideas are qualitative as well as quantitative differentials; and they are, therefore, far more efficient instruments of thought than the differentials of mathematics.

The ground of certainty for all thought carried on by means of the sensuous ideas, is the fact that the ratio of every outward object, in virtually the same relative situation, to its sensuous idea, must be the same; for otherwise the sensuous ideas would be delusive. It follows that the ratios of outward objects, in virtually the same relative situations, to each other, must be equal to the intuitively seen and known ratios of their respective sensuous ideas. An equation, therefore, between the ratio of two sensuous ideas, and the ratio of their corresponding outward objects—these being in the same relative situations—forms a proportion, any three terms of which being known involve and imply the knowledge of the fourth term.

Man, knowing the sensuous ideas and also their ratios by intuition, and knowing near outward objects also by a confirmatory bodily sense of touch or taste, can compare a near outward object thus known, or an object by inference otherwise known, with an unknown object similarly circumstanced, by regarding their ratio as equal to the intuitively known ratio of their sensuous ideas; thus constituting an equation of two ratios, or a proportion, of which the three known terms render, by legitimate inference, the before unknown fourth term likewise known.

In this way, the knowledge of concrete object after object, of concrete group after group to which they belong, and of fact after fact, in the outward world, is added to the sum of experience; and the growing, intuitively seen, synthesis of the sensuous ideas, gives assurance of a corresponding synthesis of the part of the outward world which they represent.

Great differences of distance and perspective in outward objects, and apparent in their ideas, give the basis for a conscious mathematical calculation, in simple cases, to adjust the true outward relations of those objects, by comparison with other objects; and for an instinctive calculation in cases of great complication.

When the perfection and rapidity of man's instinctive action, without the incumbrance of words and of tools, as evidenced by the construction of his body, by his immediate combined speculative and practical action, is considered, with the fact that the axioms on which the whole system of mathematics is built are few and self-evident; and with the further fact that even every dumb animal habitually puts these axioms in practice in its simplest acts of locomotion, when steering to avoid objects in its way, or to reach distant objects by circuitous routes, or when measuring the distance it can spring on its prey; the resulting conclusion, to say the least, is probable, that the isolated individual man does in fact work out in practice by his instinctive action the very complicated and very difficult mathematical problems necessary both to triangulate his course in his daily walks, and to measure and compare the mathematical relations of the outward objects by which he is surrounded.

Likewise, between sensuous ideas, viewed as qualitative differentials, there may, by analogy, be qualitative ratios, leading to qualitative proportions and conclusions. For example, by observing the ratios between the sensuous idea of a specimen orange, which I have in my hand, and have smelled, and tasted, and the idea of another object hanging on a tree, or held in my other hand; and by noticing whether this ratio is one of equality, similarity, or great difference, I can infer the same ratio between the orange in my hand and the other object; and, accordingly, that this other object is, or is not, another orange, having or not having, the same, or similar, taste, fragrance, and juiciness.

Cognition is an integral process of predominantly speculative action or thought. It involves intuition, comparison, judgment and inference, as its modes and factors, all acting successively, though seemingly at the same time, in one indivisible cognitive act; and it is aided in observation and experiment by practical action, when it needs it. For instance, the sensuous ideas are observed by intuition; their ratios are comparisons; the equations of ratios of the sensuous ideas with ratios of their outward objects, forming proportions, are judgments; and the conclusion to the fourth term of a proportion from the other three is inference.

Cognition may embrace matters of fact, as spirit, life or action, matter, existence, coexistence, sequence, causation, resemblance, difference; and also modes of being, or qualities. Cognition of the sensuous ideas is immediate; all other cognition is mediate, by means of them.

To conceive an object is to note and group the main or characteristic qualities in its sensuous ideas, and consequently in the object itself. Its concept or notion is the sum of these qualities. A general concept or notion is the sum of the qualities common to a group of sensuous ideas, and therefore to the outward objects they represent. A category is a universal concept comprising the quality or qualities common to one of the few largest groups into which all thinkable things have been divided. It is a conception of conceptions.

The act of forming general conceptions effects the organization, or incorporation, or collection, of the sen-

suous ideas in groups by the spirit for the further processes of its thought. It musters and brings together as
a whole those which are particularly or nearly related.

These general conceptions, which are also notions,
may be only used on a single occasion, or they may, if
found convenient, be habitually reformed and used; and
when they correspond to natural kinds or familiar classes,
there is no difficulty in doing so.

Categories, therefore, are not "forms of the understanding," or particular modes, or predetermined results
of the spirit's action; but, like other concepts or notions,
of which they are only the most general, they are groups
of attributes or qualities variously combined in cognition
by different philosophers; and they may evidently be
formed by instinctive thought without language, as
doubtless they are by many of the unlearned, to serve
their daily needs of thinking.

Cognition, with its notions, concepts, and categories,
embracing objects and groups of objects, with their qualities, is then extended to the motions of objects; and is
applied in all its forms to matters of fact, all of which
have some reference, through time, to motion.

When we come to consider the practical action that is
involved in, and associated with cognition, or speculative
action, we will then learn the true nature of qualities,
and find that space and time rank first among them, and
are not so-called "forms of sense." We will see, as we
may now state, by way of anticipation, that all the puali-
ties of matter are results of some spirit's action upon it;
that all the so-called qualities of spirit, of its life, are
modes of its action; that by its action all original motions

of matter are caused, and that its actions are indicated by these motions.

15. By means of the sensuous ideas, both in instinctive and in conscious thought, we know things as they are in themselves. For, in the first place, the different sensuous ideas from the same sense, and from different senses, confirm each other in the knowledge they respectively convey; and this knowledge is further aided by the spirit's practical action, as by handling, weighing, and measuring their respective objects; or by analyzing these, or other specimen objects, into their elements. And then, in the next place,—for the same reason that the ratios of outward objects to their respective sensuous ideas must, under the same circumstances, be always the same; and that the sensuous ideas by their ratios, therefore, must convey true knowledge in respect to the ratios of the outward objects themselves,—the knowledge of outward objects, in other respects, imparted through the sensuous ideas to man's spirit must be true; that is, it must represent the outward objects as they are in themselves. Otherwise, the forces rayed from outward objects upon the sensuous ideas, and marking them to guide in thought the action of man's spirit, through the bodily organization or mechanism by which it acts, would only serve as a system of delusion, inconsistent with the rational and benevolent order of the universe.

Kant says all knowledge is the product of two factors, the knowing subject, and the external world. He omits the third, the true mediating factor, the sensuous ideas. These, in their concreteness and synthesis, furnish the unity of conception, and the general conceptions.

Phenomena, or perceptions, or presentations, are not an unconnected manifold in experience; because they are conveyed by the sensuous ideas, and the sensuous ideas represent adjacent parts of the universe until they are distinguished from each other by voluntary abstraction, and then each represents a concrete object, or a definite concrete part of an object, or a concrete group of objects; distinguished, but not separated from the general field, or continuum from which it is abstracted; and phenomena are not more manifold than their sensuous ideas.

There are no antinomies in instinctive thought, or in the conscious thought that is exclusively guided by the sensuous ideas. For the intimations that come directly from the outward universe to man's sensuous ideas, serve, when carefully apprehended, only to guide, and not to mislead, his thought. When to an observer the sun appears to rise, although it is in fact the horizon that is sinking below it, the erroneous appearance is occasioned by the observer's omission to consider his own motion as that of the earth on which he is carried; just as a traveler in a railroad car, or in a boat, seems to see the trees, the houses, and the hills rushing towards him, until he re- members that it is he, with the car or the boat on which he is riding, that is rushing past them.

The conscious beginning of knowledge, or the awaking of consciousness, as we have traced it to the time when the spirit, attracted and taught by the changing marks in its sensuous ideas, looks out beyond the body, must early have become self-consciousness, as a universal synthesis of cognition; combining in organic union the self and the not-self, a representative and symbolical notion of the

universe, — a notion exceedingly complicated, and therefore apparently nebulous and confused; but gradually
resolved by the spirit's power of attention into a luminous,
harmonious, and rational system; an integral or organic
whole, of distinct but reciprocally interacting parts, or
facts, constituting together the one universal synthetic
fact of the universe.

16. In this developed self-consciousness there is a
universal conception, a universal concrete notion, of all
the sensuous ideas as a whole, and of the universe represented by them, so far as man knows it. This synthetic
notion, or conception of the universe, is the objective
continuum, or the presentative continuum, of the psycho-
logist. It is a permanent background, as it were, for any
particular idea, or group of ideas, to which attention is
directed. It is a representation of the field or arena on
which every action of man is to be performed. In it
man can see all the relations of the things he has done,
or is doing, or proposes to do. In it he can see all the
present, and in the present, all the past as its cause, and
all the future as its effect. In it also are found the parts
of man's experience already in original, synthetic, close-
combination, which Kant strove to find, and only failed
to see because he applied a destructive analysis instead
of a conservative analysis, to man's original, universal,
integral, synthetic notion of the universe.

This synthetic notion, representing the one universal
fact of a universe framed with all knowledge and truth,
reflecting and imparting them to man's intelligent
inquiry, may be divided by abstraction, analysis, classification, and generalization of its sensuous ideas into

many separate systems of sensuous ideas, corresponding to the partial facts which they represent, respectively, of concrete outward things; but it will always, by means of these ideas, collectively considered, be reflected again in its concrete form from its original, and return as a whole for the deliberate investigation of conscious and of instinctive thought. When recalled, it always represents and keeps in view the universe as a rational system, or the " kingdom of God." The conservative analysis of this synthetic notion, when aided by outward, practical action, is, both in action and result, scientific observation, experiment,—in a word, experience.

17. The conservative analysis of the original synthetic notion of the universe alternates with the artificial synthesis, or construction of its parts in thought. Thus, after the synthetic notion of the universe is analyzed, the sensuous ideas composing it are separately reviewed, marshalled, classified, brought under genera and species by the integral action of the spirit; and by their arrangement in this way each class, when consciously or instinctively perceived and distinguished, is constituted an intuitive, conscious, or instinctive, conception or notion.

This forming of conceptions by the arrangement of the sensuous ideas into classes, collective bodies, selected masses, may be regarded as the grouping of them for the convenience of simultaneous general views. This proceeding may also be called Induction, when the group or class thus formed is assumed to contain all the individuals that possess the observed common characteristics of the class or group;— while Deduction is the process by which any individual recognized as belonging to any group is held to possess all the common characteristics of that group; and by which any group noticed as comprised within a larger group, is held to have all the common characteristics of the larger group.

Thus, the one integral and universal synthetic notion, or microcosm, reflected from the one integral fact of the universe by means of the sensuous ideas, and representing as well as expressing all the real, both spiritual and material, constitutes the whole domain of philosophy. In the interpretation of this notion, by means of the first principle, all philosophy, and all the physical and all the philosophical sciences, metaphysics, logic, psychology, epistemology, ontolgy, cosmology, ethics, theology, will combine to rationally explain the ultimate nature of the universe; and will leave it better understood, in their joint result, as a rational system.

CHAPTER II.

MAN'S original philosophy, or first thought, even after he came into conscious relations with other spirits, first without language in natural society, then with language in artificial society, was instinctive and normal; so, at first, were both natural and artificial society, until ancient artificial society, by the lapse of man's thought, through the abuse of language, into idolatry, and of his practical action, through idolatry into crime, became abnormal as the union of idolatry with crime, and was called *ancient heathenism*.

18. So far we have considered the spirit of man as an isolated individual. We are now prepared to regard him as he stands in conscious relations with other spirits. We will see that, when he comes to have these conscious relations, he enters upon a higher and wider sphere of speculative and of practical action; and that his practical action affected by his conscious relations with other spirits greatly extends the scope of his speculative action; while this, in turn, advances his practical action in dignity and importance.

Now, looking out from his isolated position, by means of his sensuous ideas, upon the outward world around him, and judging, from the motions caused in his body by the immediate action of his spirit, that all original motion is caused by the immediate action of some spirit, he sees numerous material moving objects of many different forms; he observes that each of these objects of a certain form exhibits a somewhat similar series and system of motions; some of these objects being stationary and rooted in the soil, and displaying their motions in growing, leafing, flowering and fruiting; while others move about from place to place, some on the land, some in the water, and some in the air; each performing the peculiar system of motions belonging to its kind. And he concludes that each of these objects is moved, like his own body, by an individual spirit dwelling within it.

Among these moving objects he notices some with forms like his own, performing similar motions, and these objects he infers to be inhabited by spirits like his own spirit, and to be his fellow-men,—his equals. The rest, with their various forms, vegetal and animal, and with their diversified systems of motions, he concludes to be inhabited by spirits inferior to himself.

19. Then, grouping the sensuous ideas of all these moving objects, he forms a universal conception of them as the world endowed with spirit, or with life—as the living world; and, when he further observes that each of these objects is possessed of members or organs to facilitate its motions or actions, he views this universal conception as that of the organic world.

Afterwards, furnished with the universal conception of the organic world, he groups the rest of his sensuous ideas, representing the rest of the outward material universe, into another universal conception, embracing them as signifying the inorganic world.

Each of these universal conceptions would be a collective sensuous idea; and it could be used with facility in thought, by means of some smaller group, or single sensuous idea, either belonging to it as a remarkable feature, or framed by the imagination, for the purpose of representing it. Indeed, general ideas may be viewed as the solemn dolls and serious playthings of the mind, the happy work of the imagination, relieving the labor of thought; and, while differing probably from each individual, yet performing the same symbolic office for all of a class.

20. Now, contemplating the inorganic world, by means of its conception, or collective idea, as a whole, man perceives in it, too, a general system of motions or laws, or principles, the so-called laws of nature; and, by the analogy of the other systems of motions which he has observed, he is constrained to assign as the cause of the laws of nature one superior spirit, and to regard them as uniformities of his action.

Of this superior spirit, called God, man, by means of his sensuous ideas, has the same kind of knowledge that he has of his own spirit. Man knows his own spirit by his predominantly practical action or work, aided by his speculative action or work; both of which, constituting his actual life, he sees, by means of his sensuous ideas, to be realized together in the forms and motions of outward matter; and he concludes from these, as others may also do, what are the true character and attributes of his spirit. In the same way, man infers the being with certainty, and also, though liable to some deception, the probable attributes and the apparent character of the spirit of his

fellow-man. In the same way also, when relying solely
on the sensuous ideas, and not misled by the antinomies
of language, and in a case where no deception can be
presumed,—man proves, by a strictly logical demonstration, the being or life, and the true character of the
spirit of God, from the general system of the forms and
motions, or laws, of the inorganic world; which must
necessarily proceed from the action of spirit, and, owing
to their uniformity and vastness, from a single superior
spirit; and which must be necessarily designed to effect
the very complicated system of useful, and benevolent,
and ennobling ends for man's benefit and education,
which they actually accomplish.

Man infers the omnipresent action of the superior
spirit in all parts of the material universe from the
simultaneous presence and action of his own spirit in
all parts of his body—performing thousands of bodily
motions at the same moment.

21. Before proceeding further in the investigation of
man's speculative action, we will review, to some extent,
his conscious as well as instinctive practical action from
its concrete beginning in the outward world. Man's
early individual practical life, after his birth into the
outward world, is consciously as well as instinctively
devoted, in the first place, to the nourishment, shelter,
and defense of his body. In these operations he experi-
ences sometimes aid, sometimes opposition, from the
spirits or lives of plants, of animals, and of his fellow-
men, all engaged in caring for their own bodies; while a
bountiful supply of materials for their construction is
provided for all from the inorganic world by God.

In fact, it is evident from the analogy of the action of man's spirit in constructing his body, that the spirits of plants and of animals, in regard to their bodies, do the same; and that the bodies of man, of animals, and of plants, are all built up by their respective spirits, out of materials furnished to them for this purpose from the elements of the inorganic world. These elements are manifestly prepared and fitted for this use, through the laws of nature by God, as that superior spirit who is seen to exhibit in the forms and motions of the inorganic world the benevolent character, as well as the power of his action; and who, by allowing for this use unstinted stores of the inorganic matter which he controls, and works up for this application of them, displays in a marked and particular manner his unselfish and disinterested goodness.

There are certain fluid elements, as air and water, that can be directly taken from the common stores of inorganic nature, by all plants, men, and lower animals, by breathing and imbibing them, and are thus utilized for their bodies; water forming the greater part of their bulk in men and animals, and carbon, a constituent of the air, composing a large proportion of the bodies of plants. These fluid elements are so abundant that no opposition is experienced, and consequently no effort or enterprise, in most cases, is required for appropriating whatever portions of them any individual organism can use.

But there are certain mineral elements, equally necessary for the construction of the bodies of plants, of man, and of the lower animals; but which only the plants can directly take into their bodies from inorganic nature. To obtain these mineral elements for the use of their bodies, herbivorous animals consume the bodies of plants; and carnivorous animals for the same purpose consume the bodies of the herbivorous. Man, with the same end in view, consumes the bodies both of plants and of animals.

Plants always yielded up their bodies for man's use, without resistance, for clothing, for weapons, for boats, and for his domestic structures, as well as for his food. Animals, from the beginning, defended themselves against him. Some also assailed him openly, others secretly, by surprise and stratagem, thus teaching him self-defense and the arts of offensive war; while others, as the ant, the bee, and the beaver, gave him lessons in co-opera-tion in the industrial arts,—lessons of great value in man's early history.

22. Thus, the plant life and the animal life, by which man saw himself environed in the outward world, and the necessity experienced by him to defend his body against hostile attempts, and to seek for the support of his body those indispensable elements that are only to be found in a condition suited for this use in the bodies of plants and animals,—led to the exercise of practical labor and in-dustry, with skill, energy and foresight by the individual man, in order to accomplish those ends. Then, the further pursuit of the same ends led him to form con-tracts or agreements to realize them as common social ends by the association, community, or society of man with his fellow-man. Accordingly, in order to more effectually protect himself against carnivorous animals,

also to hunt and kill, or to capture, collect, and herd animals, and to cultivate plants, useful for food, he was early induced to form associations with his fellow-men beyond the family for mutual advantage in such designs.

In this way, human society began to extend beyond the family; and with the extension of society there was produced a vast enlargement of man's speculative views, and of the scope of his practical action. But, before entering upon a discussion of his social relations with his fellow-men, it is proper to notice a circumstance growing out of his relations to plant life and animal life; and which affords a clue to the solution of some mooted questions concerning the elements of his knowledge. These questions can be rapidly disposed of.

23. Man is distinguished from all other animals by the fact that he cooks his food. The importance of this fact is, that man by his practical action changes the natural qualities of the material objects he uses as food, and imparts to them new artificial qualities. Now, if man can superinduce qualities on matter, it follows that God can do so. And if no other cause is known, or can be found for the qualities of matter, it follows likewise that their cause is the action of God. We are free, therefore, to think of matter as being originally pure, without any of what we know as its natural qualities, and to consider it as carefully prepared by God with qualities adapted to man's senses; cooked for him, if you please; or distilled and condensed in Nature's vast alembic, from floating nebulæ.

Quality, therefore, is the adaptation of matter to the apprehension of man's senses, and a fitness of it for man's use. The adaptation and the fitness are not evolved, but are the deliberate results of God's action, which are seen in the laws of nature.

24. Owing to the small size of the sensuous ideas, and the great number of them ever present which the spirit can conveniently contemplate at one time, it can use directly in forming its judgments and inferences its groups of these ideas, instead of the notions, conceptions, and imaginative symbols it has constructed to represent these groups. In order to explain the sensuous ideas by contrasting them with language, something of the nature of language will be here anticipated, before we come to treat of the uses of language in society.

Language, as we shall see, is a contrivance of man to externalize the sensuous ideas, their groups, symbols, notions, and conceptions, in plastic, oral, written, and mimic signs, for the purpose of communicating, recording and preserving his thought in society. But, even when most verbose, it is an extremely abbreviated, rude, and imperfect short-hand notation of the immense number of the sensuous ideas, and the groups of them, actually used in original thinking. It vainly seeks, by its abbreviations and condensations, to overtake the marvelous rapidity of instinctive thought. Sometimes, therefore, its terms connote abstractions and complexes that instinctive thought, in the same connection, does not always need to employ; and sometimes they fail to connote important parts of the fact they are designed to denote.

25. Space, time and gravitation, are among the terms whose definitions, in language, present difficulty. Space is a compound quality of matter, its most general quality, belonging to every particle of it; and it consists of the three simple qualities of length, breadth, and height, the three so-called dimensions. Its universality, as apprehended by spirit, implies the universality of matter, and of motion in the inorganic world, as all matter known is in motion; and it therefore also implies the universal presence of God's spirit, as the cause of all original motion of the inorganic world. Time is a compound quality of action, and therefore of motion, which is caused by action; and it consists of the simple qualities of present, past and future; rendering action a train, or series, as the co-existence and the sequence of sequences or changes. Every action, whether in thought or in the outward world, produces an effect, a change. The change produced on outward matter is motion. The change produced by the spirit's action in thought on the sensuous ideas, is their analysis and synthesis in trains, corresponding first to the sequences of events in the outward world, passing or present; then to their causes or antecedents in the past; these trains being supplemented by links of imaginative ideas, projecting the effects or sequels of the present into the future, and the whole thus produced being qualified as a continuous time line of action, or chain of causes and effects, reaching from the remotest known past, through the present, to the most distant future. The time line of action is measured from a known era by known units of motion, involving and representing assumed units of time,—the

yearly orbit of the earth, the monthly orbit of the moon, and the daily revolution of the earth,—the latter multiplied into weeks, and divided into hours, minutes and seconds.

Gravitation is the continuing, original, calculated combination of forces, constituting the action of the spirit that impelled condensed matter into our system of the universe, and resulting in the known compounded motions of this matter towards the several centers of that system.

Space, time, and gravitation may be considered, instinctively, without language, in the vast system of the sensuous ideas, in a general view that will give support to the tendency of modern physical science to represent "all physical phenomena as modifications of motion."

26. In the absurd conflict that has hitherto been carried on between science and religion, based in a great measure on the antinomies and paralogisms due to the abuse and inefficiency of language, and especially to the term infinite, which has no single or collective representative in the sensuous ideas—it has been forgotten that although ignorance still places limits on the advance of science as well as of religion, science, while decrying the alleged ignorant mysteries of religion, has invented for itself, as its boasted prerogative, mysteries still more incredible.

For, although the defective terms of language, when relied on as instruments of thought, convey only imperfect knowledge of Nature and of God, the sensuous ideas, being far more perfect instruments of original thinking, impart to the spirit in instinctive thought, for the reasons already given, correct knowledge of outward material things as they are, and through them, for the same reasons, the true knowledge of God. The mysteries, therefore, that false science, whether idealism or agnosticism, has contrived by denying the reality of the noumenon or thing in itself, or by admitting its reality and denying all knowledge of it, and by asserting the inscrutable nature of the power, called God, which it confesses to stand, although unrevealed, behind the operations of nature—are as weak and superstitious as any mystery of religion. Nor do the idealists and agnosticists fail to admit, accordingly, that their mysteries, or dogmas, are instinctively rejected by all mankind. The mystery of materialism, or a world without spirit, is virtually identical with the mystery of idealism, or a world without matter; matter and spirit being used interchangeably in these scientific mysteries.

If it should be objected to the reality of the sensuous ideas that, although they are plainly visible to the spirit, they are not laid open by the dissecting knife, the answer is, that their matter may be as impalpable as the material ether which is supposed to pervade the universe, and still to be matter.

27. It only remains now to show, before considering man in general society, that in the primitive family he was capable of acquiring without language, by means of his sensuous ideas, the rudiments of that faith which, when developed in society by true education, is the highest liberal culture.

Faith means the action of man's spirit when energized by divine influence. As the action of man's spirit is both

speculative and practical, there is a speculative faith and
a practical faith. The method of procuring divine influence upon man's spirit is by his study and application
of principles, which are the rules or uniformities followed by God's action in the laws of nature. They are
speculative and practical.

By the study and application of speculative principles,
as those of scientific truth, man is exercised, educated,
and disciplined in the manner of God's speculative action,
or thought; and his spirit by this communion with God
is intellectually energized; as it is even by frequent intercourse with a fellow-man of superior intelligence; and it
thus acquires speculative faith. Similarly, by the study
and application of practical principles, as those of love
and justice, even in the primitive family, man is exercised, educated and disciplined in the modes of God's
practical action, and his spirit is thereby practically
energized; and it thus acquires practical faith.

When man entered into society, therefore, before his
invention of language, he was, as this invention proves,
not meanly endowed.

28. We have now come in the course of our inquiry,
to consider man's social life and the mutual relations
of that social life and artificial human language.

Man's practical and speculative social life, integrally
connected, as exhibited, first, without language in primitive, or so-called natural society, and then in the artificial society formed by means of language, will therefore
next claim our attention.

29. The concrete beginning of all normal human
society is the family. Its absolute beginning, like every

absolute beginning, lies beyond the scope of our investigation. The male and female members of the first family or families, if there were more than one family at first, were associated by a practical common covenant made with each member for their common benefit, by the superior spirit, God; and initiated by his promise, symbolized by the rainbow, that the laws of nature, so long as man conforms to them, will continue to act uniformly for the benefit of all men. The acceptance by man of this promise, by habitually making use of the laws of nature, and acting with reference to them, completed the covenant as a contract between God and man, and implied man's assent, and virtually his promise that the laws of nature will be utilized by him in the way God intends them to operate; that is, not only for the individual benefit of man, but also for the common welfare of all his fellow-men, who are all equally the objects of God's care.

This covenant between God and man is the original and continuing social contract. God's promise, man's acceptance of it, and its resulting binding obligation, are all proved, on one side, by the continuance of the uniformity of the laws of nature, and their manifest purpose; and, on the other side, by man's intelligent use of them, and by his social arrangements whose avowed object is the general welfare.

30. Man's earliest intercourse with animal life and plant life tended to develop his normal practical action, his moral nature. In his conduct towards animals, as fellow living beings, although not human, yet serviceable to him, he might exhibit the rudiments of morality in

kindness and gratitude. Animals domesticated for his use claim from him a gentle and forbearing as well as firm treatment, devoid of cruelty and of unnecessary harshness. In opposing formidable or noxious animals, he learns the duty he owes himself, to defend his rights of person, with prudence and resolution, against violence and oppression. There are also moral considerations in man's conduct toward plants. While their use and consumption as necessary, is allowable, their wanton destruction, or abuse, may be immoral. The removal of forests may render, as it probably has rendered, extensive regions of fertile country comparatively barren, and it may therefore become a public crime. Careless or negligent cultivation of plants necessary for human subsistence, by those who have undertaken it, is manifestly blameworthy.

The obligations of man resulting from his relations to animal life and plant life, impose on him rudimentary moral duties. Some of the obligations of man to outward animal life are expressed by the statistics of the extensive interests involved in animal culture and the fisheries; to plant life by the mere terms agriculture, gardening, horticulture and floriculture; and to both animal and plant life, by the clothing he wears, representing the vast textile manufactures of wool, cotton, flax and hemp. Now, all these obligations, showing the dependence of his life on outward living things, and awaking in him the theoretical sentiment of thankfulness to them, although he lacks the power to repay their benefits, prepare him for the grateful experience of his indebtedness to the help of his fellow-men, and for actually reciprocating, by his services, as he has the power to do, their helping practical love.

31. But, it is in human society that the moral obligations of man to man under the original and continuing social contract, which may be simply called the social contract, arise. They demand for their ascertainment the highest speculative action of man, and for their realization his purest and most energetic moral practical action. For their discharge requires the fulfillment by him of the social contract, and, for this purpose, its investigation and a review of the laws of nature, which it binds man both to study and to utilize, as well for his fellow-man as for himself.

The laws of nature, as we have seen, are the uniformities of God's action, as manifested in the motions of the inorganic world. They are called, when apprehended as conceptions by man's spirit, Principles; and the uniformity of the uniformities of God's action, or the whole interrelated system of his action, as an integral whole of action, may be called, when apprehended by man's spirit as one complex conception, the First or highest Principle, from which all other principles, as its integral parts, may be deduced.

The First Principle is the highest principle at once of knowledge and of practice,—of the speculative reason and of the practical reason; that is, of the integral action of man's spirit.

The laws of nature, and the first principle which includes them all, exhibit not only the variety, and energy, and scope of God's action on inorganic matter, but also both his wisdom or intelligence in guiding that action, and his moral character in determining the relations of his action to the spirit of man. The first principle, therefore, exhibiting the moral character of God for man's imitation, involves the whole moral law.

32. There are five elementary activities, both of individual and of social life, constituting five distinct common or universal social ends; which are, education, religious service, industry, charity, and government. The extreme complexity of society arises from the fact that each individual takes part, in different degrees, in each of these elementary activities. But, as the instinctive practical action of man's individual spirit, guided by his instinctive thought, constructed the amazingly complicated and wonderfully perfect organism of his individual body, so the combined instinctive practical action of man, associated with his fellowman by the original universal social contract, which includes in the first principle the moral law, gradually built up, in the lapse of ages, under the guidance of his instinctive thought, by means of his sensuous ideas, the still more complicated instinctive mechanism of the normal universal society of mankind.

This society, even in its primary form, must be regarded as an integral whole; each of its individual members being engaged, in different degrees, in each of the five elementary social activities as a common social end. The conservative analysis of the primary universal society, therefore, must be based on these five elementary social activities, and must be purely ideal, exhibiting five integral parts corresponding to them. These integral parts of society are its five Integral Organs, each devoted to one of the primary social activities. All these integral organs, therefore, are numerically identical; each as integral interpenetrating all the others. Just as the same body of individuals may constitute at the same time a school, say, of philosophy, a church, an industrial association, a charitable corporation, and a local government; all exercising their different functions either successively, or, if at the same time, then by separate representatives for each separate function.

This early society being natural, or without language, and its shifting, roving, wandering groups of individuals and families being, respectively, like the atoms and molecules of a fluid body, tended to become unstable, and to have its loosely cohering elements constantly arranged and re-arranged in ever varying combinations.

Yet, it must be regarded, from the beginning, as an undenominational association of all the integral organs; each of them being considered as a separate social denomination in theory, while all of them are simultaneously and indistinguishably active in practice. But in the natural course of the development of society each of its integral organs would be subdivided into partial organs, and these into smaller associations, each devoted to the special care of one of the particular social interests, involved in one of the common social ends. The lowest of these subdivisions, in each integral organ, would then require a certain permanency in the association of its members, for mutual support in its practical work; and would establish permanent primary local neighborhoods, and thus gradually localize and solidify society.

The instinctive organization of society, established by the original and continuing social contract between God and man, is based on the first principle; and, so far as it is the co-operation of all the primary social activities, it is like that principle, which is the co-operation of all principles. It is the undenominational germ of society, an undenominational association, involving all the social activities and interests that tend to the individual and the general welfare of man. Its integral organs will re-appear, further developed by language, in artificial society, as the separately organized, independent, co-ordinate, and numerically identical republics of letters and art, of the church, of industry, of charity, and of government. For natural society, after the invention of language, became artificial society.

But the normal development of the original undenominational association of natural society, by means of language and of the principle of the division of labor, into normal artificial society, cannot be traced in history. It can only be inferred from the historical development into modern civilization of the undenominational association of Jesus and the twelve disciples, by means of the revived principle of representation, as will be seen hereafter. Before Christianity, there were seen in historical times, outside of the great heathen monarchies, only single tribes under patriarchs and chiefs in various parts of Asia, Europe and Africa, except twelve tribes occasionally loosely united in Palestine under a judge; and only single cities in Asia Minor, Arabia, Africa, Greece, and Italy, under different kings; the kings in the cities of Greece and Italy, being for a time super-

seded respectively by separate democracies or aristoc-
racies. The great despotic monarchies were consolidated
by conquest. But nowhere, before Christianity, could
tribes or cities be seen united by representation into larger
political communities.

Nor can the origin of language, by means of which
natural society was converted into artificial society, be
historically traced. Something of the nature of language
has already been anticipated. We now proceed to its
uses in society.

33. Language is a system of sensuous ideas external-
ized by means of conventional, oral, graphic, plastic or
mimic signs. Prayer, or the communion of man with
God in instinctive thought, by means of the sensuous
ideas, probably first suggested language. This communion was carried on with the sensuous ideas, because
God, being omnipresent and omniscient, could know
them while they were within man. But instinctive
thought could not be communicated by man to his
fellow-man by the sensuous ideas alone, for one could
not look upon them in another. Hence, appeared the
obvious necessity to externalize them, by signs representing them by representing the objects which the ideas
represented; and by other conventional signs, indicating
the relations and motions of those objects.

Language as the body of conventional outward signs
of the inward sensuous ideas, by gestures, sculptures,
paintings, cries, oral and written words,—is perhaps
man's most important invention, and it doubtless required many centuries to obtain approximate perfection.
But no language can fully represent the innumerable,

individual, concrete, sensuous ideas. Nor can language successfully compete, either in the speed or the certainty of reaching results, with the sensuous ideas.

The superiority of the sensuous ideas compared with mere verbal descriptions, is evinced by the effect of object lessons, practical experiments, plans and diagrams, in teaching physical and mathematical sciences. A verbal description of a physical object, as a plant, an animal, or a mineral; or a verbal demonstration of a geometrical theorem, as that the square of the hypothenuse of a right-angled triangle is equal to the sum of the squares of the other two sides, would convey a very inferior degree of knowledge compared with the effect either of a specimen of the physical object, or of a diagram representing the steps required to prove the theorem. The sensuous ideas which the names of the physical objects and the statement of the theorem would produce, would probably be either altogether false, or indistinct and confused; while the sensuous ideas resulting from a view of the specimens and of the diagram, would be clear and distinct.

By far the greater part of thought, therefore, continued from the first, as it still continues, to be instinctive; and only its final or partial results, and not its intermediate processes, are what language concerning any subject matter was first used, and is still chiefly used, to communicate. Hence language was invented to communicate, but not to supersede, the instinctive thought that is carried on by means of the sensuous ideas.

For the social contract imposes the obligation, not only to learn by solitary instinctive thought, but to use,

in common with others, and for this purpose to communicate, to teach, the laws of nature, or the first principle; and the society formed by the social contract
requires the frequent communication of a common end
or object, as can best be done by language, in order to
form the various co-operative associations that constitute
society.

Language, from the first, therefore, was chiefly useful
in furthering agreements, contracts, and associations
among men, by expressing through signs intelligible to
them all objects proposed for their common assent or
pursuit. It was in this way that society, by the employment of language as an artificial means of communicating thought for its development, became artificial.

There is no ground for assuming that in the primitive
society, before the invention of language, called natural
society, the action of man, however limited or imperfect,
became abnormal or immoral. The rise of moral evil,
and of abnormal social action, must be sought, as will
be explained hereafter, in artificial society. The separate
beginning, however, of artificial society cannot be exactly
defined; because, while language was the means by which
artificial society was made, it was artificial society that,
by its agreement, established the significance of language.
Hence, the concrete beginning of each is the simultaneous concrete beginning of both.

34. The rise of abnormal action, or of moral evil
and intellectual error, may be traced to the abuse of
language in artificial society; moral evil being the result
of intellectual error, and language, as an imperfect
human invention, being suited to communicate either

truth or falsehood; while the marks imprinted on the
sensuous ideas by the forces of nature can only express
the truth of facts.   Not only antinomies and paralogisms, but also all false doctrines spring, not from the
sensuous ideas, but from the unskilful manipulation of
language.

Moral evil results, not from the erroneous teaching
of mathematical or of physical science, but from imparting a false intellectual conception of the character
of God.   For the man that is taught to know and that
does know the true character of God, as the impersonation of truth and goodness, power and love, knows also
that he is in God's immediate presence; and in that
presence his unfeigned reverence and awe, with all that
is noble in his nature, are called forth, and he does
not dare to think evil, or do evil, even if he could.
On the other hand, when man is taught to regard God
as an idol, or an immoral monster, he gathers courage
from the imagined example of his idol, as its devoted
follower and worshipper, to commit all the evil to which
his own unbridled passions tempt him.

It seems probable, therefore, that moral evil, or the
abnormal moral action of individuals in early artificial
society, originated in idolatry, or resulted from it; as this
did from imperfect and misleading forms of language,
misdescribing God's character; breaking up the potent
unity of his perfect personality into a weak assemblage
of comparatively insignificant, personified, individual,
divine powers and attributes, associated with personified
and deified human crime; forming a grotesque, abomin-
able hierarchy of vile and wicked sun gods, moon

gods, star gods, bird gods, fish gods, beast gods, and snake gods, besides monstrous so-called good and evil spirits. Figures of speech, however innocent they now are, doubtless aided, in ancient times with other forms of language, to establish idolatry.

The scene in the garden of Eden, purporting to describe the origin of moral evil, shows both the abuse of language in a statement giving a false character of God as untruthful, and the resulting idolatry of Adam in believing that statement — a belief amounting to a departure from the God of Truth, and to the acceptance, in his stead, of a false idol. For the attribution of immorality to God creates, in his stead, an idol of the imagination.

Much time was required to elapse after man's invention of his powerful mechanism of language, before he learned, if he has yet learned, to use it with absolute safety in his highest concerns. Hence it would be well to inquire, whether the greater part of the crime prevailing in modern civilization is not due to the widespread Oriental doctrines taught there, assigning to God, by an abuse of language adopted from heathenism, a cruel and immoral character.

35. But, however idolatry originated, its absolute and almost universal sway over ancient society, and its transformation of that society into the system called ancient heathenism, or Orientalism, is undoubted. For the original social contract and its first principle, with the instinctive organization of the primitive universal society, discovered by instinctive thought, were gradually reduced by idolatry and man's consequent abnormal

practical action, except in the faintest outlines, to utter oblivion and neglect.

The transition period of society from the original undenominational association of primitive normal natural society, through the first stage of normal artificial society, before idolatry set in,—to those loose and promiscuous combinations of individuals and families that are found along with idolatry at the beginning of history, and were then subject to the mere customary rule of patriarchs or chiefs, supported by the influence of idolatry, in single independent tribes,—preceded all historical records and monuments.

Only a myth or tradition of this period has come down to us. This transition period of society is what we may suppose to be meant by the tradition of the Golden Age. Because it was before the introduction of idolatry and of moral evil, it must have been a season of peace, unvexed by war. Its peaceful growth would partially develop its integral organs in local neighborhoods; and its localization would render its habitations permanent, and free from the disturbance of nomadism. Its masses, not being driven together and concentrated by conquest, or domineered over by military rule, must have been kept together in quietness and order by the deliberate adoption of positive laws; which, in the absence of any so-called political superior, or despot, must have been enacted in the form of express contracts or agreements; and these, when extending over large territories, must have been negotiated and concluded by authorized agents or representatives of the people, although no trace of such ancient representation has survived.

But, after some unknown lapse of time succeeding the supposed normal period of artificial society, the begin-. ning of history records a very marked degradation of society, shown by nomadic wanderings, occasional conflicts, and resulting offensive and defensive wars of single tribes, under their respective patriarchs, against each other. Then, the elevation of a successful military leader in these wars as king over a tribe, instead of the patriarch; and the conquering wars of the king subduing and plundering tribe after tribe, and reducing them under his dominion, driving the population of conquered districts in herds, as slaves, to his capital, until he established, as king of kings, a vast predatory and conquering despotic empire; to be in turn shattered and broken in pieces by a mightier conqueror, is the often repeated outward history of the East. The despot superseded the patriarch.

The patriarch was both the political ruler and the priest of his tribe; and the despot succeeded to the patriarch's authority in both capacities. Thus was established the system of idolatrous despotism, or ancient heathenism, otherwise called Orientalism.

To complete the picture of ancient heathenism, or Orientalism, its religious and domestic economy must be considered. To its outward military despotism must be added the description of its inward sacerdotalism, and the resulting slavery of its people.

The patriarch, the king, and the king of kings, were supported in their political rule by the priestly office. The patriarch was his own priest. The king or despot employed a company or order of priests, a sacerdotal order for the support of his authority over the people.

Institutions must be judged by their own characters, not by the characters of their casual incumbents. There have been in ancient times good patriarchs, good despots, and good priests, as goodness was accounted in their day. Abraham and Melchizedek were model patriarchs, but they did not originate patriarchism, which arose long before their time in idolatrous nations. Marcus Aurelius, the Roman despot, who lived thousands of years after the reputed author of despotism, Nimrod, was a Stoic philosopher; and although he conscientiously persecuted the Christians, he was notoriously endowed with all the Stoic virtues. Early Jewish history reports some good priests, but they disappeared in the glory of the prophets.

A good patriarch or despot might allow and proclaim a God of justice and mercy. But a heaven-daring conqueror, making it the occupation of his life to form, and when the occasion offered itself, to execute plans for ravaging and laying waste extensive territories, and visiting with indiscriminate slaughter or slavery their unoffending populations, would not permit himself to be insulted by the worship of a just and merciful God. After the shining example of Nimrod, he allowed his creatures the priests, to proclaim his divinity. He would then through his priests, his sacerdotal order, command the worship of a wrathful, cruel, and unjust idol despot in heaven, to countenance the unjust and cruel despot on the earth.

He thus systematically debased his fellow-men, by enforcing the unworthy worship of himself, and of an idol like himself, as fellow-gods. For the series of ancient conquerors were a race of men as exceptionally strong in intellect, as they were wicked and unscrupulous in practice, and they well knew that a God of love, and mercy, and pity for the people, is only suited to a democracy; while the cruel policy of despotism, conquest, and slavery, required the superstitious, supernatural support of a wrathful, unjust and cruel idol.

In fact, the sacerdotal order in the despotism of Orientalism, or ancient heathenism, did as much to degrade and brutalize men, and fit them to become loyal and submissive subjects of the despots, as did the armies which the despots employed for that purpose.

For this order, by its support of the despot's power, earned from him the unlimited privilege of plundering the people by pretended mercenary religious services; and it stimulated the willingness of the people to bribe them for these services, by further debasing them with degrading superstition, first intensified by multiplying and diversifying their idols, and then utilized by assuming an official and confidential relation to these idols; and by asserting the ability to placate their wrath and win their favor, by sacrifice, the universal ceremony of idolatrous worship.

Nor should it be forgotten that in ancient heathenism, or Orientalism, the same merciless cruelty of the ruling classes to the people, was exercised, when the people were submissive, by those classes towards each other, and their own members, and even by the nearest relatives.

Thus, it appears that, by the system of ancient heathenism, the light of humanity was almost extinguished; mankind, with few exceptions, having been degraded into two classes of beasts: beasts of burden, and driving or ruling beasts. For, by this system, when idolatry and abnormal action became predominant, the instinctive germ of social organization, based on the native dignity of man as the image of God, on the original social contract of God with man, and on the first principle, was thoroughly overthrown, broken up, disintegrated, and superseded. The order in which the ruin of the integral organs of society took place, after they had been partially and symmetrically developed, according to the five primary individual and social activities, and had been, to some extent, duly localized by local neighborhoods or associations, must have been as follows: first, the functions of the integral organ of the republic of government were usurped by the despot; secondly, the functions of the integral organ of the republic of the church were usurped by the sacerdotal order; thirdly, the integral organ of the republic of industry, as an association of freemen, was crushed by the despot and the sacerdotal order, by means of the universal slavery of the masses of the people; fourthly, by the same means, and the consequent universal misery of the masses of the people, and the isolation of the ruling classes from them, the integral organ of the republic of charity was rendered impossible as a public institution—although charity was not entirely obliterated by slavery, there having been at Rome, as is proved by tender inscriptions still to be read in the Catacombs, charitable associations, as for burial, among the unhappy slaves; and fifthly, the integral organ, or republic, of letters and art, was restricted, by the same means, either to the sacerdotal order alone, or to it along with the rich, learning having been monopolized by these classes, and no public education in which the poor could share having been established.

Ancient heathenism, or Orientalism, founded on despotism, idolatry, sacerdotalism, and slavery, was a virtually uniform system. Its primitive form, with very little variation of its essential features, dating from the mighty hunter of men, Nimrod, whose memory, to awe mankind by his pretended divine example, was enthroned by superstition and kingcraft in the brightest constellation of the Northern skies, Orion, has been handed down in regular succession, through the despotic and conquering monarchs of Chaldæa, Assyria, Media, India, China, Persia, Parthia, Egypt, Greece, Imperial and Papal Rome—for the temporal power of the Pope is despotic—to the present Grand Turk, and the Tsar, with his Oriental Tartar rule of to-day.

The system of ancient heathenism, or Orientalism, grew to be as universal as it was hideous and monotonous. Normal artificial society was altogether obliterated by it. Only an individual, here and there, remained, upon whose heart was written the law of God, and who led a normal life; testifying to the power of instinctive thought, when duly heeded, in the most unfavorable outward circumstances, to sustain man in the intimate communion with God, and to derive from that communion the energy of speculative and practical faith.

Doubtless, many such individuals, oppressed by slavery and despotic cruelty, lived in obscurity, and perished unknown. But a few others have achieved the brightest fame of history, and have indicated, amidst almost universal despotism and idolatry, the glory of humanity. Such were Pericles, Demosthenes, Socrates and Plato among the Greeks; Abraham, Moses, and the prophets, among the Jews; the Gracchi and Cicero among the Romans; Buddha, and perhaps Confucius, in the East.

But the name, in the splendor of which every other name of man must pale, is that of a child, whose birth in a poor and isolated family, in Bethlehem of Judea, is the new era, from which the revived normal artificial society, or the new Golden Age, called modern civilization, is dated.

CHAPTER III.

THE doctrine and the practice of the Kingdom of God, being the revival, by Jesus, of normal artificial society from ancient heathenism, by means of the revival of the speculative side, and the consequent revival of the practical side, of the original or Semitic Philosophy.

36. We will now inquire by what means, and how far, normal artificial society was first revived from ancient heathenism in modern civilization, or Christianity; what is its natural constitution, as revealed by instinctive thought; what steps backward it has taken in reaction towards ancient heathenism ; and what, afterwards, has been the course of its progress and reform, in its symmetrical normal development.

At the birth of Jesus of Nazareth, the system of ancient heathenism, or Orientalism, in the despotic and coterminous empires of Rome and of Parthia, virtually covered the whole of the then known world; extending in the Roman Empire from the Atlantic to the Euphrates; in the Parthian, from the Euphrates to the farthest East.

The Greeks had gloriously, but vainly, resisted and defeated at Marathon the entrance of Oriental despotism into Europe. For afterwards they succumbed to it under one of themselves, a conqueror who surpassed the conquests, and adopted the despotism, of the kings of the East—the Macedonian Alexander, whose empire, in turn, was conquered, and whose despotism was imitated, by the Romans.

Thus, despotism and idolatry, as the system of ancient heathenism, or Orientalism, were established throughout the known world, with the exception of the few persons on whose hearts was written the law of God.

But the idolatry of the Roman Empire was not all polytheistic. For the great body of the widely dispersed Jews held fast, with wonderful heroic obstinacy, to the doctrine of monotheism, which they received from Abraham. Yet, it cannot be denied that the object worshipped by the majority of them was not that God of justice, mercy, and love proclaimed by their great prophets; but rather the popular ideal of a mighty and ferocious conqueror, whom they expected to batter down in blood and carnage, either in person or by a Messiah, the hosts of Rome and Parthia, and to divide their spoils among his favorites, the Jews.

The savage and cruel being whom they imagined and worshipped must be classed among the idols of imagination; and their worship, as monotheistic idolatry.

The idolatry, therefore, that prevailed, along with despotism, throughout the known world, at the birth of Jesus, was both polytheistic and monotheistic.

The monotheistic idolatry of the Jews arose from their degrading the character of the true God of the original pure monotheism of Abraham to the level of the behavior of the cruel chief idols worshipped by the heathen nations. It was the monotheism of the Jews that gave them the power of resistance against the ineffable oppressions which they suffered from successive conquerors for thousands of years, and that enabled them to survive all their oppressors; but it was these oppressions that degraded and obscured the spirit of the Jewish people, and thereby caused the majority of them to lower their estimate of the character of God. Yet, there always remained, mostly in humble circumstances, a few who did not bow the knee to Baal, and among them, occasionally, a great prophet.

It should cause no surprise, therefore, that in the general darkness of idolatry and despotism that had overspread the world, a young Jewish villager, who, at the age of twelve, was carried by his zeal for the knowledge of the true God to the feet of the great teachers of his faith, in the Temple of Jerusalem; and who, by questioning the travelers that regularly passed his door at Nazareth with the great caravans from the far East to Tyre, Sidon, and Egypt, had opportunities to know all the forms of idolatry, and to learn the need of the world for enlightenment, should be inspired by the thought that the great Deliverer expected by his people must be a great enlightener; and should recognize in the consciousness of his own great power of thought and of expression, a call to assume that providential office for his day. For he saw that an enlightener or reformer of the world, necessarily beginning his reformation by instructing a small circle of pure monotheists, could most easily establish that circle among the Jews, already monotheists, by purifying their monotheism.

It was, accordingly, the monotheism of the Jews that as a Jew he first purified; so that as in its original purity it was made the foundation of Christianity; and it became, after his death, the vehicle for spreading Christianity, by means of the Jewish synagogues, scattered throughout the Roman Empire.

37. For it was necessary on account of the monotheism of the Jews, although it was in some respects impure, but prevailing among no other people, that a Jew should become the reformer of the polytheistic idolatry of ancient heathenism.   It was necessary for him to begin his reform in his own country, among his own countrymen, and in his own neighborhood, among his neighbors; in order that he might at once—in the brief period that his enemies would allow him—bring together, instruct, and inaugurate in action, a small association inspired by a pure monotheism, as a type of a new and normal artificial society, a present example of it, and as a germ or nucleus for future development.

As the original normal artificial society must have been at first undenominational, and was as such overthrown by idolatry, it was fitting that the revived normal artificial society should at first also be undenominational, and should be founded on the overthrow of idolatry by a pure monotheism; while the development of its social denominations, or separate integral organs, must be left to be called forth by the exigencies and opportunities of the future.

The only way to remove error, is to teach the truth. The only way to remove the error of polytheism, with its related despotism, was to teach the truth of monotheism. To do this effectually it was apparent that—in order to produce an immediate and lasting effect on the vast heathen world—a band of zealous monotheistic teachers, missionaries, or apostles, was required who could be prepared for their mission in a short time. Such a band young Jesus, at thirty years of age, in his humble sphere of life, could only expect to find among the Jews,—his countrymen, his neighbors. ‐These were already monotheists, prepared in that aspect to his hand. It only remained for him to select willing and able associates among his humble acquaintances; to purify their monotheism from some common prejudices, regarding their expected Messiah, and the true character of God; and to instruct them for their mission in the short time at his disposal.

There was every reason why Jesus should seek in his great mission his associates among the Jews. The monotheism of the Jews had separated them from all the peoples with whom they came in contact, who were all polytheists; and it had thereby made the associations of individuals and families among the Jews more sympathetic, more close, mutually more helpful, and more lasting, than among other non-Semitic nations; and thus it preserved the inward cohesion, and consequently the national vitality of the Jewish people; while in the calm of these domestic associations the idolatrous features of their monotheism would find nothing to call them forth; and the true character of God, revealed by instinctive thought and the sensuous ideas, and preached by the prophets, would at least dimly shine forth, and—so far as it was apprehended—would ennoble their intercourse, and give strength to their character. Their Mosaic institutions of civil law surpass in humanity any of the ancient heathen codes.

38. In the way thus pointed out, Jesus of Nazareth, as a Jew, began at his home, among Jews, his reform movement. It is recorded of him, in books that are almost universally conceded to be authentic history, that he was born in Bethlehem, of Judea, of poor Jewish parents, his father being a carpenter; that in childhood he was taken to Egypt, and then brought to Nazareth, of Galilee, where he lived until about thirty years of age, when he began a public ministry of teaching, by proclaiming what he called the "Kingdom of God," or the "Kingdom of Heaven"; that he carefully instructed twelve men of the common people, and formed them into an association with himself, to spread his doctrine of the "Kingdom of God," and his association, among the people; and that, after a public career of about three years, preaching his doctrine with unexampled genius, eloquence, prudence, and intrepidity,—besides ministering charitably to all whom he met afflicted by sickness,—he suffered on the cross a heroic martyrdom for the cause he had advocated, saying of his doctrine, in almost his last utterance, that he was "born to bear witness unto the truth."

39. By generously consecrating his young and pure life to the witnessing of the truth, he made that life its best witness, the true interpreter to all noble and sympathizing minds, of the formula "Kingdom of God," in which he summed its comprehensive import.

The most eloquent of men, he distrusted the power of written language to adequately express the doctrine which he taught for all mankind, and for all time. For this reason he left nothing in writing. He committed his doctrine to the perfect instinctive mechanism of the sensuous ideas, aided by the oral tradition of his discourses.

He simply addressed oral speech to the common people, to awaken their instinctive thought, and to call their attention to the systematic action and Providential care of God, manifested in the observed order of the universe. From the order of the universe, as the action of God, he drew the character of God, as the perfect ideal of goodness, love and wisdom, for man to imitate. He thus left all questions as to his doctrine to be answered for him by God as the supreme oracle in the temple of the universe.

It will be more appropriate here to develop briefly the intrinsic meaning of the formula, Kingdom of God, in which he condensed and symbolized the whole import of what he taught, than to needlessly dwell on the convincing collateral testimony and authority which his life, as credibly reported, and already universally known, gave to his teaching.

40. The formula, Kingdom of God, may be converted into the proposition, The Kingdom is of God. When Jesus proclaimed the formula, Kingdom of God, he asserted as a truth, that the Kingdom is of God. The sensuous ideas of the conception and of the assertion are the same. Now, in order to understand the

teaching of Jesus, the meaning of the two terms, king-dom and God, must be clearly ascertained.

The term God meant, in that formula, the God of pure monotheism, as already described; the one superior spirit of power, wisdom, goodness, justice, and love, far exceeding any attainment of man. The term, king-dom, meant concretely, the organization, order, or sys-tem produced in anything by the action of spirit, and abstractly the power, authority, or guidance of the spirit that produces the organization, order, or system.

The term, Kingdom of God, then, meant, concretely, the organization, order, or system, resulting in the material universe from the immediate action or power of God, and in the spiritual universe, and in a particular and primary sense among men, it denoted the normal society effected by God's instruction, discipline, and example, co-operating with the action of man. When the term, Kingdom of God, does not plainly mean the whole material and spiritual universe, it means the organization, the order, the co-operating union, associa-tion, or society of God with mankind.

The term, kingdom, connected with the term God, cannot mean anything implied in human government. Such a meaning given to the term kingdom, in this connection, is an abuse of language, involving gross error, and leading to the most disastrous results; to an idolatry tending to thrust back modern civilization into all the evils of ancient heathenism. For the applica-tion of the term king to God in any sense implying functions of command analogous to those of a heathen king or despot, or any other human, royal prerogatives, is simply idolatry.

Indeed, the conception of government between God and man, is absurd as well as idolatrous. Government inflicts punishment as an evil to make retribution for another evil. God inflicts no evil, and therefore no punishment. He administers discipline as a blessing; in order to lead the offender to repentance and reformation. God is the rule for man to live by, to measure and direct his conduct, not man's ruler. If God should issue a command as a ruler or absolute king, it would be known to whomsoever it might be addressed, from one end of the universe to the other, as the still, small voice; and man could not fail to obey it. But his obedience would be a mere matter of necessity, and it would have, therefore, no moral value in his eyes or in the eyes of God.

Man is in the power of God, dependent on his gifts and his guidance. God is at once his loving father, friend, associate, and his skilful employer, teacher, trainer,—in the school, in the field, in the workshop, and in the arena of life,—and man can only show his gratitude to God, by doing his duty and giving his assistance to his fellow-man, and thereby doing the work of God. For God asks of man no tribute of empty praise, or idle, sentimental love, or vain or costly sacrifice to him,—but calls on all to lend a hand and aid him in his work of universal blessing to mankind. The spiritual relation of man to God, is that of a scholar to a teacher, of a free apprentice to a just, wise, and good employer, and of a practical helper to God in bestowing his beneficence.

The heathen depravation of God's character, by the attribution to him of heathen governmental functions, and of corresponding heathen acts, analogous to those of a human despot, or king, judge, or military leader, was the chief heathen or idolatrous element of the monotheism of the Jews. But the term kingdom, in the formula Kingdom of God, excludes every function of government. It merely designates the organization, order, or system of the material and spiritual universe, and particularly of normal society.

This meaning of the term kingdom, in the formula Kingdom of God, will be further elucidated by the signification which Jesus evidently attached to the terms king and kingdom, when applied to himself and to his association with his disciples. For when he was called king before Pilate, he openly admitted the fact; but said that his kingdom was not of this world, meaning that it was not a government at all, as all real kingdoms of this world are, and that it certainly was not a revival of the Kingdom of David, which was unquestionably a real kingdom of this world; and this answer, with the reasons he gave for it, satisfied Pilate, who would not have dared to tolerate any government opposed to Cæsar, as a rival kingdom of this world in Judea, and least of all a revival of the famous Kingdom of David. Jesus was directly charged by his accusers before Pilate, with setting up a government as king; but Pilate evidently thought him innocent of the charge, and said so; and yielded to his fears for himself in condemning Jesus, and not to his judgment, as he publicly confessed, by symbolically and ostentatiously washing his hands, to remove the guilt of the condemnation from his conscience, according to the form of his superstition.

Jesus, in fact, never exercised any governmental office, and never performed any governmental act. In the only recorded case of his being sought to act governmentally, he expressly and publicly declined to do so, when called upon to divide a disputed inheritance—an act that would have belonged to a king or a judge, as governmental functionaries of a human government. The term king, therefore, as used by Jesus in relation to himself, must merely signify that he was the chief, or master of his disciples. The word translated king, in the text in question, denotes a master—as the master of a house or of a school; and it has, indeed, many more meanings, from signifying a heathen god or monarch, to a mere term of complimentary oɪ flattering address to any person admitted for the occasion, or feigned, to be a superior.

Hence, the kingdom of Jesus, which he expressly said was not like the heathen kingdoms, which were governments, was merely the organization of the association of his disciples, which was an undenominational association, and of which he was the unquestioned head, or chief, or master, but without any governmental function or authority. Nor can it be doubted that the term Kingdom of God must have an analogous meaning, denoting only the organization, the order, and the system, of the material universe, and of normal society.

In confirmation of this view, the passage may be referred to, in which Peter is called, by Jesus, the rock on which his church—as the term for it is translated, or, as it may be otherwise called, his community—shall be built. The transaction is narrated in the usual figurative style of the time; and it probably means that Peter was then appointed, or foreordained, to succeed Jesus as the future head, or chief, or president of the first Christian community. Afterwards it appeared that he was followed by James, when the first Christian community settled in Jerusalem; and that each of the other Christian communities, as they arose, had a separate head, not called a rock, but a bishop. Now, the bishop, as the head of a separate Christian community, did not, so long as it was undenominational, take the place of an apostle, but a place analogous to that of Jesus; not the place of a mere religious teacher, but the charge of the general interests of the community. But there is no pretense of any political government in any of these chiefs of the early Christian communities for more than a century after the death of Jesus. The term kingdom, then, in the formula Kingdom of God, must evidently be taken, as it is used in other connections, in a figurative sense. As a class, an order, or system of things, as of plants, is called a kingdom, so the Kingdom of God must signify, in a general sense, the system of the universe, and, in a particular sense, the system or organization of normal society, of the society based on the social contract, and in which man is the associate of God.

41. It would be no easy task to state all that is implied in the formula, Kingdom of God. This task will

not here be attempted. But a brief summary of what it implies may be given. The formula, Kingdom of God, has been already considered, on its speculative side, as implying the system of Semitic philosophy; and it will now be viewed, on its practical side, as implying the perfect instinctive conception, or ideal, of the organization, or practical constitution of normal artificial society. Both sides constitute an integral whole, of which each is an integral part; so that its speculative side is only predominantly speculative, and its practical side only predominantly practical.

Leaving, therefore, as already sufficiently explained, the speculative side of the Kingdom of God; the mechanism of instinctive thought, with the sensuous ideas; the laws of nature as the uniformities of God's action, and their sum as the uniformity of the uniformities of his action, or the first principle; with the moral law, as the moral features of God's action towards man, involved in the first principle; we proceed to the social contract of God with man, as determining, in connection with the primitive individual and social activities of man, the perfect organization or practical constitution of normal artificial society, or modern civilization.

42. The primary activities of man are derived from the first principle, being copied from the action of God towards man. God instructs man, communes with him, furnishes him with the materials of his food and clothing, aids him in his trials and necessities, and exercises over his conduct a wholesome discipline, designed to lead him to repentance and reformation. In all these particulars, man engages, by the social contract, to imitate,

towards all his fellow-men, the action of God, by utilizing the laws of nature, which God provides; each man
utilizing them both for his individual benefit and for the
general welfare of all.

Thus, corresponding, respectively, to the five primary
individual and social activities of man, which may be
called education, religious communion or service, industry, public charity, and government—there necessarily
arise under the social contract, and are instinctively
formed, five universal associations, as integral organs of
society; in each of which every individual is a member
more or less actively engaged, and all of which, practically co-operating together, constitute the organization of
normal artificial society.

For the original and continuing social contract, as
already stated, made and proved by acts, consists, on one
side, in the inferred engagement of God to continue the
uniform operation of the laws of nature for the common
benefit of all men; and on the other side, in the inferred
engagement of man, when he accepts the use of the laws
of nature, to use them in the way they are obviously
intended to be used.

It follows, that in every social relation every individual is bound to make his own interest consistent with
the general welfare; and that in every normal association
God is virtually a member concerned for directing its
common end in harmony with the benefit of the whole
community. Man has very important duties to himself
to discharge; so has every association, and every community to itself; but these duties, when properly understood, must conduce to the well-being of the public.

The five integral organs of society, or social denominations, as they may be called, have each, respectively, one of the primary social activities for its common end; and as every man must to some extent be engaged in all these activities, he must belong to all the integral organs. Hence, every integral organ must embrace all the people, and all the integral organs must be numerically identical, co-ordinate, and independent.

Each of the integral organs, therefore, must be a republic, and must be organized by subdivision into appropriate partial organs, or associations.

We have seen, that the original primitive or natural society, that preceded artificial society, must have been, at first, undenominational, holding, as a germ, all the social denominations, or integral organs, undeveloped within it; that afterwards these integral organs must have been to some extent developed; although, as this development took place before the commencement of history, its extent cannot be exactly determined; and that when history begins to throw light upon society all the normal social denominations or integral organs have disappeared, under the influence of idolatry, leaving in their place only an abnormal despotic government, and an abnormal sacerdotal church; these two abnormal institutions constituting the system of ancient heathenism, or Orientalism.

43. We have seen, also, that Jesus began his reform movement for the overthrow of ancient heathenism, or Orientalism, by establishing, as the first typical Christian community, or germ of the new society of modern civilization, which he inaugurated, an undenom-

inational association of twelve disciples, with himself at
its head.

It is from this germ, and by the influence of the
formula, Kingdom of God, implying and perpetuating
the perfect instinctive conception, or ideal, of the organization of normal artificial society, that the five social
denominations, or integral organs, which in their full
normal realization must constitute perfect modern civilization, or the true Kingdom of God, here and hereafter,
have been already to some extent partially developed,
after many vicissitudes and obstructions from the
unyielding power of ancient heathenism. Passing over
the details of the outward history of this development,
we will aim to follow its inward genesis.

In the first place, it is plain, that with idolatry both
sacerdotalism and despotism were removed by Jesus from
the type which he instituted of modern society.

The removal of sacerdotalism from the new society
introduced freedom of thought from the slavish bonds
and from the temporal power of superstition, by separating science from the dominion of false religion. It
gave to true religion the enlightenment of true science
by making both co-ordinate. It committed the interests
of science, with the care of all principles, as included
in the first principle, to the predominantly speculative
integral organ, the republic of letters and art; while it
assigned the service of God, or the preparation of man
for worthy communion with him, here and hereafter,
in immortal life, as the peculiar charge and duty of
religion, to the practical integral organ, or republic, of
the Church.

For this boon to science, as well as to religion, and for the encouragement, among the masses of the unlearned people, as well as among the learned, of original thought, by entrusting the development of the fundamental principles of science and of religion, involved in the doctrine of the Kingdom of God, to the freedom, the mathematical and logical precision, and the instinctive mechanism of the sensuous ideas when used, with the aid of oral speech and of tradition, in the instinctive thought carried on in silence and seclusion by the common people, Jesus, as the Emancipator both of science and of religion from priestly rule, deserves the highest honors, both as the perpetual chief of the republic of letters and art, and as the founder of the republic of the universal, pure, spiritual, practical, and free catholic church.

The effect of removing despotism, or the abnormal centralized state, all absorbed in an abnormal centralized government, from the new society, was to replace despotism by a normal decentralized state, consisting of three separate and independent integral organs, each charged with one of the primitive social activities, or social common ends. These integral organs are, first, the integral organ, or republic of industry, restored to independence from the despotic interference of the government in all purely industrial concerns. Secondly, the integral organ, or republic of public charity, emancipated from the obstruction of government, and needed to purify, liberalize, and harmonize public social intercourse, by æsthetic, literary, and scientific public entertainments; to smooth over and overcome by its aid the temptations, difficulties, partial disasters, and disappoint-

ments, arising from the operations of nature, and the
competitions of society; to alleviate misfortunes, and to
promote moral reforms. And, thirdly, a decentralized
and simplified integral organ, or republic of government,
confined to purely governmental functions, exercised by
the people through their representatives, as a civil
representative democracy; and aiming chiefly to secure
the public defense, to maintain public order, to enact
needed governmental positive laws, and to administer
justice in the courts.

Thus, by the removal of the abnormal systems of despotism and sacerdotalism, constituting together ancient
heathenism, or Orientalism, that had overspread the
known world, Jesus brought into play the five integral
organs or social denominations that together compose,
by their co-operation, the normal organization or constitution of modern civilization. But this result, although
undoubtedly due to the genius of Jesus, and embraced
in his vision and design of the future Kingdom of God
on the earth, was not effected at once.

44. In fact, almost the only normal outward development of the early Christian communities, while they held
fast to their pure monotheism, was their system of representation, according to which they each sent representatives to meet in a general council, for the consideration
and dispatch of their common concerns. But this system
was most important, being the mechanism by which the
extremely complicated normal organization of each of
the integral organs and of society, as a whole, can be
brought into an orderly and practical system; and being
the means by which the several Christian communities

came to be considered together as having the unity or catholicity of one Christendom.

It must be borne in mind that, as in the primitive natural society, so also in the type of modern society instituted by Jesus, the integral organ of government, on account of the absence in both of idolatry and moral evil, was only potential; Jesus, the head of modern society, having absolutely refused to perform any governmental function. Where there is no moral evil to be coerced, government would plainly be superfluous.

But the advent and increase of moral evil logically tend to produce the realization of government, and to stimulate the activity of its functions; while, obversely, from the rise and multifariousness of government may be inferred the growth of moral evil. Nor can it be doubted that the augmentation of moral evil, in the absence of polytheism, indicates as its cause the influence of monotheistic idolatry, or the worship of an imaginary being, with an immoral or cruel and unjust character, instead of the just and loving God. For moral evil is the effect either of polytheistic or of monotheistic idolatry.

45. Now, about the beginning of the third century, a sudden and ominous portent made its appearance in all the Christian communities. As if by common consent, they almost simultaneously adopted sacerdotalism and despotism in the place of their primitive constitutions. They had evidently determined to fight heathenism with its own weapons. The influence of Orientalism, or gnosticism, had prevailed.

A revolution was made in Christendom by a ring composed of a banded few, calling themselves the clergy, to subvert the growing organic Christian system of civil representative democracy, and to substitute for it the heathen systems of subordination, and of arbitrary usurpation. The clergy claimed to be the privileged few, the superiors of the people, who were called the laity, and were merely their subjects. The clergy formed themselves into a sacerdotal order, a hierarchy, and their head assumed to be, with their support, an Oriental monarch, a despot, under the name of a bishop, in every Christian community.

Outwardly, Christianity had relapsed into ancient heathenism. The revolution of reaction was completed, confirmed, and perpetuated by substituting the awful heathen religious ceremonial of bloody human sacrifice, represented in a mimic show, for the tender memorial service of the last supper instituted by Jesus.

Corresponding to this sacrificial ceremonial, typifying the injustice and cruelty of the being to whom it was offered, the sacerdotal order adopted Oriental dogmas and mysteries, concocted in the fertile imagination of the idolatrous East, couched in delusive and unfamiliar forms of speech, but interpreted by the sacerdotal order to sustain its ambitious pretensions.

Combinations of bishops in provincial councils, formed inner rings of the sacerdotal order, and a union of all the bishops in a general council, completed the ecclesiastical machine, the head of which became the bishop of Rome.

46. The ecclesiastical machine of Christianity had, after the labor of a century, in the year 325 A. D., undermined the authority of the avowed heathen sacerdotal system in the Roman Empire; when the heathen

emperor, Constantine, who was at once the head of the heathen sacerdotal system as its Pontifex Maximus, and of the military machine of the empire as emperor, conceived the practical plan of securing for himself the powerful support of the Christian ecclesiastical machine by a compromise of its impure monotheism with the shaken and effete polytheism of the Roman sacerdotal order. Accordingly, Constantine, with a view to such a compromise, proposed a conference with the Christian ecclesiastical machine, which met him in full force in a general council at Nicea; and over which he presided as the heathen Pontifex Maximus, representing the polytheistic element of the empire. The result of the conference was the adoption of the so-called Nicene creed, one of the conflicting Oriental or gnostic dogmas that had invaded Christianity from the East; and which the shrewd imperial Pontifex Maximus foresaw would easily admit of a sufficiently idolatrous interpretation to satisfy the entire heathen element of the Roman Empire; although he was somewhat vexed and disappointed to find that it did not receive the unanimous support of the bishops.

Soon followed the irruption of the barbarous and idolatrous masses of the Roman Empire, with their gross superstition, into the Christian church, or the so-called conversion of the Roman Empire; and the Christian ecclesiastical ring was elevated at once to a pitch of opulence, splendor, pomp, luxury, and power, unsurpassed by any sacerdotal order in the most idolatrous ages and populations of the East.

47. From that time to the present, as logical results of the prevailing impure monotheism of Christianity, the Christian ecclesiastical ring or machine, representing the Oriental sacerdotal order, on one hand, and the Christian military machine, or military government, representing Oriental despotism, on the other hand, have almost everywhere, with occasional prudent relaxations, or necessary exceptions, outwardly dominated the unresisting masses of the people, in the larger part of what is called modern civilization. But the final frustration of the ecclesiastical machine's attempt to subdue the state under the church by its claim of temporal power in Europe, has saved the people there from a worse than Mohammedan rule.

Of the crimes of the ecclesiastical ring, which is also the model of the military ring, I do not propose here to speak; but of its errors, or rather of its one fundamental error,—its impure monotheism, or monotheistic idolatry, from which all its well-known historical crimes and persecutions have proceeded,—it was necessary that something should be said in its proper place. In the criminal rivalry of the church and the state for supremacy over each other, the state was as guilty as the church.

In the Roman Empire the Christian church and state were only partially separated. The emperor arrogated much authority over the church. Theodosius made a law punishing heresy with death. Some judicial authority was granted to the bishops, and they usurped more, thereby intruding on the functions of the state; but not more grossly than the state had trespassed upon the

functions of the church.   In this respect the church and
the state of Christianity were equally heathenized.

48. Having shown the outward career of Christianity to have been a sudden, early, and persistent
relapse into the system of ancient heathenism, we will
now as briefly trace its inward development.   Under the
surface of society, below the rings and classes that had
usurped ecclesiastical and political authority over them,
the common people, the descendants and successors of
those to whom the gospel of the Kingdom of God was
preached by Jesus, have always preserved, with the
formula or symbol, Kingdom of God, the tradition of
the main points of its development, as orally delivered
by Jesus to his disciples.   By means of this tradition,
they were always, and they are still, fully able, by their
instinctive thought, aided by their experience, their
sensuous ideas, and their personal communion in prayer
with God, to reconstruct, develop, and apply to present
circumstances, the doctrine that Jesus taught.

For, what Jesus taught was not a figment of the
imagination, an invention, a fantastic dream, a fiction, a
creation of his unequalled genius; but the truth, committed to him, as he said, by the Father, to be communicated to all men,—the truth of God, and as such
suited to the common understanding of all men, and
which they can find, where Jesus found it, written for
their benefit in the heart, on the face of nature, and
proclaimed in God's Providence.

It was an idle, as well as a wicked thing, for the Christian hierarchy, or ecclesiastical ring, to pretend to have
received the deposit, and to have the exclusive custody

of the true faith, as they called it, or of the doctrine
taught by Jesus.   While the people could elect their
religious leaders and teachers, these could be held in
check, and could be relied upon, to keep alive the pure
tradition of the Kingdom of God.   But when the clergy
separated themselves from the people, and formed themselves into a self-constituted body of priests, they cut
themselves off from the true line of tradition, and their
tradition became as worthless, and for the same selfish
reason, as the tradition of the Pharisees.

The claim of the ecclesiastical ring to be the infallible
church is utterly untenable, for the church is the people.

The true supernatural revelation is the First Principle,
and that is not confided to the ring; but is open to the
interpretation of every one who will diligently consider
it, and seek its instruction.   In view of the fact that the
truth of the Kingdom of God is traceable in the First
Principle, and is a common possession, which, as to
man's ordinary wants, may be utilized by all men, and
as to his higher spiritual needs may be enjoyed as a
solace by all those who have higher aspirations, the inference is clear, that among the masses of the people, a large
proportion of whom were slaves, though of the white
race, in the Roman Empire, and as intelligent as most
of their masters, there would be, in large volume and
measure, an ever renewed tradition of the comforting
doctrine of Jesus.   Nor is it probable that the Christian
sacerdotal order, who were for several centuries chiefly
concerned to mingle in the pursuit of wealth among the
rich, would attempt to inculcate their peculiar dogmas,

with the care their teaching required, upon the unprofitable poor, to the exclusion of that tradition.

49. It is not asserted, that the Christian sacerdotal order altogether ignored the popular tradition of the doctrine of the Kingdom of God; for the tradition was vouched for by martyrdoms of world-wide renown, and was afterwards reduced to writing in documents made imperishable by it, and which in turn sustain the tradition; but that this sacerdotal order made the tradition of the facts and doctrines of the true primitive Christianity entirely subordinate to the dogmas they invented or imported from the East, altogether outside of Christianity, and operating merely to support and magnify the authority and power of the order, as a self-constituted non-representative ruling body, over society.

50. After the lapse of more than sixteen hundred years from the revolution which transformed the simple and unassuming elective bishops, or overseers, of the early Christian communities into Oriental despotic monarchs, then banded these bishops, with those persons who officially assisted them in the ceremony of religious worship, from presbyters and deacons down to the door-keepers, as a clergy, into a self-constituted, non-representative Oriental sacerdotal order, or religious ring, and gradually adopted or devised, outside of primitive Christianity, Oriental dogmas, that afterwards grew into a permanent creed or symbol, tending to consolidate and perpetuate that sacerdotal order, it would be difficult now to correctly assign the motives of those engaged in the movement. It may be that the revolution met with no opposition from the masses of those communities,

composed to a great extent of slaves and of very simple and poor persons not accustomed to take part in public affairs. It may be that the increasing pressure and persecution of the heathen government seemed to make it necessary for the Christian communities, who could no longer hide their meetings in upper chambers, in grave-yards, or other out-of-the-way places, at night, to have leaders analogous to those of their oppressors, and vested with authority to enforce unquestioning obedience for the general good, in the sudden and distressing exigencies that frequently occurred.

But, whatever were the motives of those concerned in this revolution, a Christian sacerdotal order was then established; Oriental dogmas were then, and shortly afterwards adopted by it, and those dogmas have ever since helped to strengthen that sacerdotal order.

That sacerdotal order, the clergy, never burned nor otherwise tortured, in any way, any person for violating the Christian moral law,—for not paying his debts, or not supporting his family, or for any fraud or violence against his neighbor. But, if any man, woman or child, whispered, or even formulated in silent thought a doubt concerning any one of the Oriental, or gnostic dogmas, tending to maintain the authority of the clergy, they would set up a court of inquisition, that by the most barbarous and exquisite tortures and fiendish cunning would extract a confession of the *doubt,* and condemn the victim to be burned at the stake. Thus, if any person doubted the doctrine of transubstantiation, or of the real presence, or of the trinity, or of the autocracy, or absolute political power of the pope, he was condemned to be burned alive, and his property was forfeited to the clergy and the state.

The punishment of secret thought, by the Christian sacerdotal order, was a refinement of heathenism that no heathen sacerdotal order had ever imagined. The criminality of the condemnations of the Inquisition is aggravated by the fact that it blasphemously asserted that they were made for the glory of God, when in fact they were decreed for the support of the sacerdotal order. The crusades against the Waldenses of the Alps, and the Albigenses of southern France, were cruel, wholesale executions by order of the Inquisition.

To be just to the clergy, it must be stated that they did not themselves burn their victims; but only "commanded, and that under the most awful threats, that the fire be lighted, and the victim tied to the stake by others." [Milman, L. C., VII., 437.]

51. The demoralized state of Christendom stepped forward and executed the commands of the Christian sacerdotal order. In England a statute, "de comburendo hæretico," was passed under Henry IV., in 1400. In Continental countries of Europe it is believed that no special statute or law for the purpose was considered necessary, and that the governments simply obeyed the orders of the clergy in burning its victims.

The complicity of the governments, or military machines of Europe, as the successors of heathen Oriental despotism, in the abnormal action of the Christian sacerdotal order, in the matter of burning so-called heretics, is evident. This may be said of the governments of Europe

in general, Protestant and Roman Catholic; both before
and since the so-called Protestant Reformation.

52. The military governments of Europe have also
adopted the heathen governmental maxims of Orientalism—the maxims sanctioning offensive war and conquest,
and those permitting the arbitrary rule over the people
by a hereditary governing class of kings, emperors and
nobles.

53. It may be said, therefore, on the one hand, that
the primitive Christian community, inaugurated by Jesus
as the Kingdom of God, has outwardly relapsed into
modern forms of that ancient heathenism, or of that
sacerdotalism and despotism which Jesus had completely
excluded from it.   For all abnormal action, or moral
evil, as already stated, results from idolatry, and may be
called heathenism; while normal action is in accordance
with the Kingdom of God.   And it may be added that
the modern, like the ancient forms of heathenism, originate from the same cause: namely, from that mode of
idolatry that consists in attributing a false or immoral
character to God.

54. But, on the other hand, the primitive Christian
community has developed itself in partial accordance with
the doctrine of the Kingdom of God, as taught by Jesus,
into forms of modern civilization, altogether foreign to
ancient heathenism.

The Christian church, notwithstanding its sacerdotalism, has divided itself into the two inchoate, but distinct, integral organs, formerly combined in the sacerdotal church: namely, the republic of letters and art,
and the republic of the true church.   Likewise the

Christian state, notwithstanding the modified despotism of its military government, has also unfolded itself into the three separate integral organs, which were before compressed into it in the despotic state: namely, the republic of industry, the republic of public charity, and the republic of government.

The separation of the inchoate republic of letters and art, from the sacerdotal church, was caused by repeated revivals of letters; first proceeding from the Mohammedan Arabs, who soon after their conquest of degenerate Christian countries, far surpassed the Christians in literature, especially in Spain; then from the culture inspired by the wealth and industrial activity of the free cities; then from the Christian schools and universities, and especially from the study of philosophy and of the newly found civil law taught there; then from Abelard, Arnold of Brescia, and the school men; then from Savonarola, Wycliffe, Huss; then from the renaissance of the study of the Greek classics on the fall of Constantinople; and then from the invention of printing and paper.

The sacerdotal church attempted in vain, by the Inquisition and by the crusades against the Albigenses and the Waldenses, to check the advance of learning and of liberal thought, which it correctly supposed would undermine its sacerdotal authority. But the inchoate republic of letters and art defended and saved, as it must ever do, the cause of truth.

The separation of the inchoate integral organ or republic of industry from the military or heathen state, is still only partially accomplished. The first step of the separation was caused by the remarkable revival of industry in the cities, beginning in the old Roman municipal towns of Italy, soon after the completion of the barbarian conquest of the Western Roman Empire, and extending rapidly to the cities of Spain, France, Flanders, Holland, England, Switzerland and Germany. The object ·pursued by this industrial movement, and accomplished by it in the course of centuries, was to emancipate the industrial classes from the oppression and virtual slavery imposed upon them by the feudal, which had succeeded the Roman government.

This revival of industry caused also a partial development of the integral organ or republic of public charity, by supplying funds for endowing and operating many charitable institutions and associations.

The revival of industry further affected the government, by enabling the cities to obtain their freedom, and secure it by charters, from the feudal government. This tended to somewhat mitigate the heathenism, or despotism, of the government by introducing representation from the now important cities in the legislatures of different European nations—as Cordova, France, England, Germany, and Switzerland; and by securing for a time, until grossly abused, the independence of the cities of Italy.

But it must not be forgotten, that the most reformed of the European governments, in 1350, in the reign of Edward III., retained enough of its heathen character to retard the organization of the republic of industry, by passing an act of parliament which fixed the rate of the wages of working-men, forbade them ·to contract for higher wages, and punished as crimes combinations among them to defend their rights.

55. While the disintegration of the sacerdotal church and of the despotic or military state was progressing, as above stated, a conflict between them for mastery was carried on with great vigor; the sacerdotal order, on one side, claiming supreme temporal power over the state, and the state, on the other side, claiming authority to rule the church. The sacerdotal order of the western or Roman Catholic church, by various devices, succeeded in obtaining the temporal power it sought, after abandoning the less energetic Greek church to itself, so far as this enterprise was concerned; and during the thirteenth century the authority of the sacerdotal order of the Roman Catholic church over the state in western and central Europe became despotic, and was despotically used. After that time, the temporal power of the sacerdotal order gradually declined, and by the so-called Protestant Reformation it was entirely thrown off from the states that adopted Protestantism; while the power of the people in the government gradually increased; results that may be fairly attributed to the rise and partial development of the two modern or revived integral organs, or republics, of letters and art, and of industry.

56. It may be stated, as an inference from all the preceding observations, that there is a controlling and attracting unity, and a corresponding simplicity, presiding over and ordering all the manifold variety of being, of thought, and of action, in the universe. By tracing the individual man in his examination of self-consciousness, and in his relations as well to the inor-

ganic as to the organic world, to the inferior spirits of plants and animals, to the equal spirits of his fellow-men, to the one superior spirit, God, to the laws of nature, as the uniformities of God's action, to the uniformity of those uniformities, as the one First Principle of all truth and of all normal practice, and to the one original and continuing social contract of God with man, developed from that principle; we have arrived at the unity of perfect society, as the Kingdom of God, or the association of God with man, in the one universal society of the races of mankind. Moreover, as there is only one external source of all normal human action, namely, the example of God's moral character manifested in the First Principle, so there is only one internal source of man's abnormal action, or of moral evil, namely his error or ignorance as to the true moral character of God. Leading to man's departure from imitating that character, this error is also a virtual denial of the true God, by falsely attributing to God a character false, cruel, or otherwise immoral. It is the monotheistic idolatry, which is the single cause to which may be assigned all the crime, the secret sin, and the discord prevailing, not only in ancient heathenism, but also in modern civilized society. To this fact the attention of every church should be directed.

The conclusion of the whole matter is, that, the fundamental internal cause of the moral evil and of all crime and ignorance in modern society being a single error, the nature of which can be plainly taught, which can be removed by instruction, and only by instruction, being the original and prime heresy of monotheistic idolatry, into which the sacerdotal Christian church early fell; it was to overcome by the truth of God this heresy, inducing and including all the other heresies and crimes of society, that the republic of letters and art, the pre-dominantly speculative integral organ of society, as an investigating and teaching body, entirely independent of the church, co-ordinate with it, and having the peculiar function to seek, and to teach, in the First Principle, the whole range of the principles, as well of truth or science, as of normal practice, or practical morality, has been gradually developed from the original germ of the King-dom of God. Hence, all the practical integral organs, including the church of God, entitled to be called catholic, or universal, when free from heresy and sacer-dotalism, became bound to adopt from the republic of letters and art, and to realize in practice, all their respective practical principles.

It follows that, as all the integral organs of society have the same system of laws or principles, derived from the First Principle of the Kingdom of God, by the repub-lic of letters and art, there can be only one normal order of society, constituted by those integral organs and their principles. It follows, also, as the Kingdom of God was proclaimed by Jesus as a fact, involving the system or complex of unalterable laws or principles, which, when viewed together, are called the First Principle, and em-brace all principles; that the one normal order of society constituted by the integral organs of society and their respective principles, must also be a fact within the King-dom of God, and must be detected in the actual society of mankind as its true organization, at work below the surface.

A conservative analysis, or ideal vivisection of the actual society of mankind, therefore, so far as it approximates to the Kingdom of God, must disclose the true or normal organization of that society; and the description of that organization will furnish the ideal social constitution,— as a matter, not of theory, or of imagination, but of fact.

The next chapter will attempt to sketch the actual ideal social constitution, stripped of the deformities of heathenism still adhering to it, and fitted to regulate the perfect universal society of mankind.

CHAPTER IV.

THE Ideal Written Social Constitution,—being a development of the revived, predominantly speculative, social side of the Semitic Philosophy.

57. The artificial constitution, humanly expressed, of the Kingdom of God, or of normal society, as modern civilization, and as instinctively conceived, will now be described; it being so much of the unwritten, instinctive, rational, ideal, or natural constitution of the Kingdom of God, or universal society of the races of mankind, as may, when universally assented to, and adopted by tacit or express general agreement, be established as such in writing.

All future social progress of mankind can be nothing more than the rational realization of the instinctive conception of the Kingdom of God, as outlined by the teaching of Jesus, and based not only on the original and continuing social contract of God with man, and on the first principle of all science, and of all normal practical action, but also on the five elementary and universal, individual and social activities of man: namely, public education, religious service, industry, public charity, and government.

The following articles, describing from the instinctive conception of the Kingdom of God, as the ideal

of perfect universal society, its actual organization, as
a real though embryonic fact, by giving both the common and the distinctive features of its working integral
organs, exhibit the outlines of what must hereafter be
more definitely formulated, by general agreement, as
the written, universal, social constitution.

ARTICLE I.

58. This article will give the common features of
all the integral organs of society, leaving the details distinguishing the organization of each of them, respectively, to separate succeeding articles.

Universal society is an association of associations, each
independent of the rest in all that exclusively concerns
it; all formed to promote the five elementary and universal, individual and social, activities of man; associations rising in generality from the primary associations,
composed of the inhabitants of the lowest territorial
or local subdivisions of each nation, to associations
which are national; from these to those which are international in each race; and from these to those which
are Interrace among all the races.

Each of these associations is five-fold, constituting a
separate, though numerically identical, association for
realizing, in a separate capacity, each of the five elementary activities.

The territory of each nation is parceled out into a
number of primary subdivisions, called districts, or
neighborhoods, or parishes, of a convenient size to
enable the inhabitants of each to assemble in a primary meeting of its association.

The organization of the association of each primary local district, or neighborhood, must be the meeting of all its members, or of those choosing to be present, convened at stated times, for each of its capacities; and at other times, on due notice; organized according to the general parliamentary law; adopting its resolutions by a majority vote of those present, to bind as a contract the whole association; and electing its authorized agents, or representatives.

Each higher association than a primary one, is formed for a larger territorial district, and acts by means of representatives assembled from such of the next lower class of associations as occupy together the larger district. Its resolutions bind it as contracts, and appoint and authorize its representatives.

Each nation is divided into at least one intermediate class of districts above the primary; with a co-extensive association for each intermediate district, acting by representatives from the lower districts within it, and designed to regulate, according to its several capacities, and in respect to each of the several elementary activities, the local concerns of its district, whether a city, town, county or other rural area.

If a nation is divided into larger territorial divisions, as states, or provinces, each of these should have a central association, acting by representatives from the next lower associations within it; and the nation should also have a national central association, acting by representatives from the state or provincial central associations.

If a nation is not divided into states or provinces, or other analogous large sections, it will have a central national association acting by representatives from the intermediate associations.

The organization of each association higher than the primary is representative, and it is of two kinds, called respectively, undenominational and denominational. Both of these kinds of organization are distinguished from everything heathen by employing representation as their means of co-operative action, and they are distinguished from each other by the different kinds of representation they use. These two kinds of representation may be called generic and specific.

Generic representation is the kind used by the undenominational organization; as, when all the representatives of an association are charged to advocate its general, undivided or integral interest, without partiality for any particular denomination of that interest.

Specific representation is the kind used by the denominational organization; as, when some of the representatives of an association are charged, respectively, to advocate specifically one particular denomination of its interest, and some, another. There may, in different cases, be relatively different degrees of generic and specific representation, according to the interest represented.

All the elementary individual and social activities are practiced by individuals, and by temporary associations of individuals. But these individuals and temporary associations, as members of universal society, are entitled not only to have the protection and encouragement of the whole community, or society, to which they immediately or mediately belong, but also to have the helpful guidance of wise general regulations adopted by universal agreement for the equal profit of all; and it is the duty, and should be the object, of normal society to afford this equal protection and guidance by its highest organization.

The most general associations of each nation, as well as of the race to which it belongs, are the five integral organs of society; each designed to promote, in all the races, one of the elementary activities, and having in each race a thorough national organization, which receives authority "from below," as distinguished from the despotic, sacerdotal, and feudal systems, which derive their authority "from above." Combining all the local associations having its special activity in charge, in each nation of the race, every integral organ is, in theory and potentially, international and Interrace in its scope.

The complete organization of universal society is the co-operation of its integral organs. To effect this co-operation each integral organ, besides its fundamental organization of lower local associations, must have an organization that is superior, or general, and separate from the rest; each integral organ being regarded as an independent republic.

The type of the general organization of each integral organ, regarded as an independent republic, is the system of civil representative democracy, partially realized in the general government of the United States of America.

For the integral organs other than that of government, however, there will necessarily be some diversities from some of the general governmental forms.

The government, in a military point of view, needs a chief executive officer, a head, a leader, a representative of the whole people, and co-ordinate with the legislative and the judicial departments.

The other integral organs need no chief, or leader, co-ordinate with the legislature. In each of them its highest representative body is its general legislature. The highest executive officers in each of them may be a small board of executive commissioners, elected for a short term of years by the legislature, responsible to it, and appointing their subordinates subject to its confirmation.

The general legislature, or the central regulative body, of each integral organ must form the head of an ascending scale of representative assemblies, delegated respectively, from its primary, intermediate, state or national local associations; each local association determining by its representatives the affairs relating exclusively to its locality; and leaving to the highest, or general legislature of each integral organ, the formulation of those general regulations, that relate in common to all its members, in the exercise of its particular elementary social activity. Each integral organ may have two general legislatures, one undenominational, the other denominational.

The general regulations adopted by the general legislatures of each of the integral organs, and by their local associations, must, so far as they are positive laws, be morally binding, as public contracts, on all the members, respectively, of the integral organs or other associations enacting them; and their enforcement, like that of other contracts, must be sought in the courts of the government. Hence, a judicial department in any of the integral organs other than the government, would be a superfluous piece of machinery.

The constitution of the Kingdom of God, as perfect universal society, being an infinite ideal, open in its integral generality and graded development to the instinctive apprehension of all, the description of all its minor details would be as useless at any time as it must always be impossible. Only the main features of the divine plan, as they have been already in part realized, or in the advancing progress of society have come into the near prospect of fulfilment, need be outlined. The organization of the integral organs of society, as the main elements of the Kingdom of God, will now, in succession, be separately treated.

ARTICLE II.

59. The Republic, or Integral Organ, of Letters and Art.

The elementary activity of this integral organ of society, is public education.

Its means are schools, colleges, universities, public lectures, and the press.

Its modes of action are investigation and teaching. It acts by individuals worthily assuming to represent it, and by associations. Its highest associations are its two general representative assemblies, or legislatures, one of which is undenominational, and the other denominational, in each state or nation; and from which, respectively, delegates or conference committees may be sent to some central point to meet similar bodies from the other states or nations of the same race, to form similar international assemblies or legislatures.

The subjects of its investigation and teaching are language, all the principles of philosophy, of the special sciences, and of practice, including the fine and the useful arts; all these principles being included in, and derived from, the first principle, or the system of the laws of nature, or of God. It must particularly teach manual training, and the cultivation of a healthy body,' and practical morality, with whatever else it may teach.

Its general representative undenominational legislature will be composed of representatives, themselves chosen by representatives of its undenominational, local, primary meetings, when assembled in their respective local intermediate districts; these local meetings being convened to act for the general interest of public education.

It will enact such regulations as may be necessary to direct the general affairs of the various institutions of public education it may establish.

It will also appoint two boards of Commissioners. One of these boards would be executive, called general Commissioners of Public Education, whose duty it should be to establish, according to instructions prescribed by that legislature, a complete system of public education, from primary schools to colleges and universities, for teaching all the subjects enumerated before, belonging to liberal culture. Acting also under the instructions of that legislature, local commissioners of public education, elected by the people of each locality, will have charge of the local schools.

Teachers should be appointed, according to general regulations, during good behavior, after favorable examination. The office of commissioner of public education should be honorary, and for a short term, subject to re-election.

The other board of commissioners, predominantly critical, though partly executive, would be called the Commissioners of Public Criticism. The republic of letters and art being responsible for all seemingly important publications allowed to pass without its dissent, these commissioners should be men selected for their eminent knowledge, character and skill, and suitably salaried to pass deliberate judgment, for the information of the public, as the authorized decision of the republic of letters and art, on a classified range of the most important current publications of science, literature, art, and journalism; separating the good from the worthless, however well meant, and reporting their decision to the public in a cheap periodical paper.

They should pay particular attention to the independent, general, or undenominational journals, forming the bulk of the reading of the general public, and which should furnish, with all the resources of condensation, precision, and system, a vivid panoramic representation of the present doings for the passing day, with occasional retrospects, of all the social activities.

All publications should be protected by a general copyright for a certain specified term, or until condemned or approved by the commissioners of public criticism; and after approval by them a further special copyright should be granted for the usual term by the commissioners, by their certificate specifying their approval of such works as they have favorably criticised. The commissioners should certify the works they have unfavorably criticised or condemned.

Authors and publishers dissenting from the decisions of the commissioners, would be free to appeal to the public through the courts, by applying for an injunction against reprinting a work improperly condemned by the commissioners.

The general undenominational legislature shall provide funds for the payment of salaries and other expenses incident to public education, by a small general assessment, to be limited by the Government, and by receiving voluntary contributions. It shall also supervise the investments of voluntary endowments of educational institutions.

It shall encourage original investigations, as well as teach their results.

A general representative denominational assembly, or legislature, composed of representatives from the various associations formed to promote different branches of public education, whether scientific, artistic, mechanical, moral or religious, may be convened at the instance of the undenominational legislature of the republic of letters and art; or upon the call of any of those associations, as the undenominational legislature, by general regulations, may direct; and when convened, it shall consider such of the interests or subjects of public education as may be specified in its call, and it shall report the result of its deliberations to the undenominational legislature, for its action.

As the normal action of society is a unity, or integral whole, of action, the harmony of the combined action, or co-operation of all its integral organs; and, similarly, the normal action of each integral organ is also, a unity, or integral whole, of action; so, accordingly, the normal action of the republic of letters and art is an integral unit—a consensus of every investigation towards a perfect system of truth derived from the first principle; and . a corresponding consensus of every effort of teaching towards a universal system of liberal public education, by the school, the college, the university, and the press, and equally independent of the church and the government.

But while independent of both, the republic of letters and art furnishes for the support of both, all liberal culture, the whole system of true principles, and establishes on a firm foundation the true value of the Bible, as the most ancient charter of human liberty, the sacred repository of the rational Truth that makes men free, whatever else it may contain.

ARTICLE III.

60. The Republic, or Integral Organ of the Church.

The elementary activity of this integral organ of society, the church, is public religious service. This activity serves God by serving man, in leading him into communion with God, teaching him the knowledge of God and his true moral and benevolent character. It thus renders to man the highest service. By this activity, therefore, man, voluntarily and gratefully offering himself, and graciously accepted, as God's agent or instrument, does a material part of God's work in blessing man.

It induces man to think principles as God's speculative action, or thought, thereby acquiring some of the energy of God's thought, as speculative faith; and to imitate God in his practical action, or character, thereby gaining some of the energy of God's practical action, as practical faith.

It is the immediate communion of man with God in public, without the necessary intervention of any person pretending to be an official mediator, but with the aid of all present, sympathizing fellow-men, and especially of ministers chosen by the people, or congregation, to lead in prayer, and teach the knowledge of God's character. This, when followed by subsequent exemplary conduct, is true public religious service. It does service to God, because it helps him to benefit man.

The religious experience, called by the Quakers the Inner Light and the Inward Monitor, and some mystic declarations of other sects, may be rationally explained as the true knowledge of God, derived from the First Principle, by means of the sensuous ideas and the operations of instinctive thought, independent of language.

The means of effecting communion with God, is prayer; the association with others in pursuit of it, or public religious worship; the aid of the arts; and especially full instruction as to God's character, derived from its manifestation in the principles of nature, in the events of history, and in his common providential dealings with the individual man. Of the arts, in respect to religion, poetry and music, as spiritual, are the chief; to which architecture, sculpture, and painting contribute their aid.

The republic of the church consists of all the people, and it embraces all the religious denominations not heathen in their dogmas or practices. Religious denominations in all their relations to the general church, are somewhat analogous to the political parties of the government, in that they are separated from each other by differences of opinion, and that they jointly constitute the whole people, the whole church—all uniting in holding the same ultimate principles, notwithstanding their disagreement in matters of indifference.

The general undenominational representative assembly, or legislature, of the church, for a state or nation, consists of representatives from the undenominational assemblies of its local associations. It regulates, in general, the elementary activity, the religious service, of the church, in essential points.

It is analagous to other legislatures, because it is a deliberative body designed for a free expression of opinions, with a view to agreement in some resolution declaratory of the truth, or in some decision in a matter of practice. But it differs materially from other legislatures in several important particulars.

First, it has no political power. It cannot, therefore, use governmental modes of coercion to enforce conformity with its opinions, or to punish disagreement with them. Nor can it, as a Christian body, use any of the well-known so-called spiritual methods of enforcement, which are heathen modes of superstition and idolatry, pretending to engage and enlist the wrath of an idol god to vindicate the heathen dictates of a sacerdotal order.

Secondly, the subjects of its deliberation and action are truly spiritual, as distinguished from temporal, and especially from all outward matters of the State, whether industrial or governmental, or even of public charity. It may properly discuss the means by which communion with God in public or in private is effected, with a view to improve them all. But public religion, or the public service of God, is its general subject. Private or individual religion, indeed, underlies and supports all normal life, as life is one consistent and integral whole, guided by the one First Principle that involves the principles of private or individual religion, with all other principles. And man, as an individual, can only live a normal life and serve God as he serves man. The ways, therefore, in which man can serve his fellow-man, and thereby exercise his religion as an individual, are very numerous. But the chief outward manifestation of his religion, and the one mainly committed to the charge of the church, is the public service of God, the public exhibition and teaching of the true character of God, as the just, wise, and loving Father of mankind; for the public encouragement of man by association, prayer, example, and instruction, superinduced upon enlightenment and liberal culture, to commune with him, and follow his example in private as well as in public.

Hence, the deliberations of the church in its undenominational legislatures, or councils, while aiming at agreement in essential religious truth, must be spiritual, and will charitably recognize freedom of thought and toleration of differing opinions and usages. The councils of the church, therefore, will abstain from formulating any authoritative creed; but will call on all men to find and to follow all the truth of God. They will, to the best of their ability, confute, with charity, all fundamental error; and will avoid the heathen practice of stigmatizing error as punishable or damnable heresy; but will prescribe for all error, as its only rational and religious human remedy, cogent argument and wise instruction, leaving all further remedy to the example and discipline of God.

When required, an interstate or an international undenominational legislature, or council of the church, may be formed, by sending representatives from its state or national undenominational legislatures, to meet at some central point.

The general undenominational legislature, or council of the church, may appoint Executive Commissioners to bring the resolutions of the council to the general knowledge of the people; to promote Sunday schools, as undenominational as practicable, in the various churches; and to send efficient and liberal undenominational missions to the heathen world, at home and abroad.

There may be convened a denominational representative general assembly, or legislature, of the church, as a denominational council, composed of representatives from all the religious denominations, as such, as far as possible, to exhibit and discuss from time to time, in a charitable way, the actual characteristics or differences of all the religious denominations, while carefully noting their points of agreement, and in those points of agreement making a joint search for any common elements of ancient heathenism, or monotheistic idolatry, as opposed to the simple and pure rational Christianity.

The union, at least of the Christian religious denominations, in Christian charity, the lowest degree of which is toleration, must precede, and would probably produce, the general reformation of all the monotheistic religious denominations,—a movement which would be first of all the extirpation of all the roots of ancient heathenism and monotheistic idolatry; for only after these are removed, will the truth of God have free course and unimpeded growth.

The republic, or integral organ, of the church, in its normal action, is unquestionably an integral unity of all its denominations,—the one catholic church of the one true God. For all its various religious denominations, normally seeking the knowledge of the true character of God, with a view to its faithful imitation in public religious service and in private life, as their only essential objects; while each questions its own denominational peculiarities, resolved to dismiss from its doctrine and its practice, or ceremonial, every vestige and reminiscence of ancient heathenism; the Roman Catholic, the Greek Catholic, and the English Catholic, looking narrowly to what is distinctly Roman, Greek, and English, respectively, in their religious systems; and the other denominations examining closely that which in their doctrine and practice is rather peculiar than essential,—must seriously ask themselves whether their denominational peculiarities, even if abstractly true in doctrine and formally correct in practice, as understood by themselves, have not become, by their overestimate and their unnecessary obtrusion, mere unduly magnified accidental departures from true catholicity; but are easily harmonized and freed from every mark of monotheistic idolatry, by a return to the simplicity of pure, catholic, original Christianity.

ARTICLE IV.

81. The Republic, or Integral Organ, of Industry.

The elementary activity of this integral organ of society, is industry, a term the meaning of which expands with the advance of society, and which may be regarded now as comprehending the production, exchange, transportation, distribution, and the redistribution of natural and artificial values, and as including the regulated partial consumption, or use, and the residuary savings of them.

The means by which the elementary activity of industry is carried on, are partly material, and partly spiritual. Its material means are the material gifts of nature, and material capital, both fixed and circulating. Its spiritual means are its spiritual capital, as free labor, skill, science, credit, and the so-called forces of nature, with language and the arts.

The modes of action, or the operations, of the elementary activity of industry, are extremely various and complicated; but they may be collected, for discussion, into four groups, represented by the action of the four industrial classes,—the employers, the working-men, the consumers, and the capitalists.

While it is necessary to consider each of these groups separately, it should be observed that they are, in theory, integral parts of one whole of industry; all tending, in practice, with the progress of society, to have identical interests, with diversified advantages, as the same individual person may belong to all these classes at the same time. For, when industry is properly organized, the working-man will be not only, to a fair extent, a consumer, but also, according to his skill and prudence, a capitalist, and thereby potentially, if not actually, an employer.

The industrial classes, constituting the whole people, may all be traced to the working-men. Indeed, when it is considered that material capital can only be utilized in the operations of industry by means of spiritual capital, which is entirely within the reach of all working-men by diligence and good conduct; and that the controlling elements of spiritual capital, expressed by the term credit, are daily seen to elevate working-men to the class of employers, entrusted with the use of material capital by its owners, and enabled thereby to acquire material capital, in the form of profit; it is manifest that in a normal system of industry, when the government ceases to interfere with it, and the other integral organs co-operate with it, especially the republic of letters and art, by furnishing to all a liberal education, and the republic of the church, by stimulating in all the religious and the moral impulses, there will be offered for every one, according to his skill and perseverance, a free and open career, to pass upward from the lowest to the highest employments of industry.

To a careful observer a constant series of changes in the ranks of industry will appear, even now, to take place with spectacular interest; as in a drama, in which an actor enters the first scene as a serving man, and in the crisis of the plot throws off his humble disguise and assumes the character of a distinguished personage; or as in a circus, when a horse gallops around faster and faster, like fleeting fortune, and no rider is seen; but suddenly a person from among the audience, muffled in coarse clothing like a plain working-man, stumbles into the ring, is helped upon the horse, and sways unsteadily in his seat, seeming ready every moment to fall; but at length becomes steady, shows a level head, starts to his feet on the saddle, throws off disguise after disguise, appears more and more richly dressed, as if rising in life, until at last he bursts upon the startled and admiring audience in all the glory of spangles and embroidery,—a glittering, full-blown capitalist.

The alleged conflict of labor and capital is absurd. For labor is spiritual capital, and is daily converted into material capital. After the primary distribution of the productions of industry, wages representing the share of the workingman, the relative consumption by the distributees of their respective shares determines the possession of material capital. Those distributees who consume less than they receive, and save the surplus, have this, as material capital, in their hands.

The beginnings of material capital are always in the hands of free working-men, who receive wages; as the highest honors of government, of the church, of science and art, may often be traced to the same origin. From small beginnings material capital, increasing sometimes slowly, sometimes rapidly, produces by economy and enterprise wonderful results. Working-men bent on accumulation and endowed with energy, prudence, and patience, see and utilize the constantly recurring but rapidly passing opportunities of business, adding success to success, now by inventions, now by investments, and now by prudent and skilful management of affairs

It is by the saving of material capital, year after year, that wages are paid; and that the wonderful system of reproduction of industrial values, including material capital, is carried on. For, if the saving of material capital by working-men and employers were to cease, and every man were to consume all that he received in the distribution of industrial products, the material capital already accumulated would soon be exhausted, and the industrial business of the world would stand still. The only general occupations left to mankind would be hunting and war; war for the few wild vines and fruit trees found scattered in the woods, and for the hunt-ing-grounds that would occupy the fields of present cultivation.

The division of labor caused by the great variety of industrial occupations, when a free interchange of their productions, by means of money and of commerce, is allowed, necessarily conduces, when these occupations are supported by educated intelligence and religion, not only to the present, but also to the ultimate harmony and prosperity of them all; both by encouraging the separate organization of the industrial classes, and by facilitating the saving of material capital.

It is evidently proper that all the industrial classes should be carefully organized. Labor is partially organized, and it is desirable that organized labor should be able to meet and to consult with organized capital, organized employers, and organized consumers. For this purpose, it is necessary that the organization of each of the industrial classes should be carried to practical completeness.

The organization of labor, or of the class of working-men is defective. It is founded too much on military tactics, on compulsion, on the excessive use of self-help, which in a community governed by law should only be resorted to in a case of the last necessity, and on the imagined force of its erroneously supposed superiority of numbers; forgetting that every working-man is also a consumer, and in respect to spiritual capital, if not also to material capital, is likewise a capitalist. It lacks an institution that will enable large bodies of its members to enter, backed by strong financial influence, into business relations with employers, for well-considered and lasting mutual benefit. Such an institution is the labor bank, in which the labor and the savings of a considerable number of working-men and working-women, as its members, under suitable regulations, may be pooled; so that the bank, by its officers, may make contracts for its labor of different grades, with a guaranty against strikes, taking adequate security, and insuring the payment of wages to its members; while, as a savings bank, on strict business principles, it would loan its funds, by preference, to judicious and liberal employers.

The labor banks, if prudently managed, would probably take the place of the present savings banks, and would give the working-men an influential and peacemaking standing among capitalists and employers.

But the present labor associations, though they may still have a legitimate use, whether they are called trades unions, knights of labor, or otherwise, seem to chiefly confine their attention to the most obvious interests of working-men, in respect to wages and the hours of labor; while they neglect their less obvious, but equally important, interest in the peace and harmony of all the industrial classes. Of what advantage, however, are high wages and few hours of labor, when gained by irritating threats and expensive strikes, if thereby a universal, cruel, and vindictive industrial war among the leaders and representatives of all the industrial classes is kept up; leading to stoppages, disasters, and panics in trade, which frequently throw many thousands of working-men and working-women, and in the course of a few years, even millions, out of all employment for months, and out of steady employment for years?

In normal society, in which the integral organs are separately organized, there will be a science of industrial economy, showing the organization of industry and its proper modes of action; but because there will be no interference of government with industry, there can be no science of political economy.

Nothing can be more inconsistent with industrial economy than the plan of some working-men, who, in their rash quarrel with material capital, propose to vest all property, including all material capital, in the government. For this measure would necessitate the extreme centralization of the government, with an unavoidably absolute central ruling body, like Plato's supreme council of philosophers; and would, by excluding all competition of capitalists, create a practically despotic monopoly of material capital, under the management of that ruling body, who would be the only employers, and whom all working-men and working-women would be compelled, by the whole power of the government, without resistance or complaint, to serve.

Although in normal society there could be no intentional interference of the government with industry, the right of the government to raise its revenues, in whole or in part, by duties on imported goods, can not be denied. But the integral organ of industry would have an equal right to insist on there being appended to the tariff of import duties a proviso, that, "when it shall be made to appear by a consular certificate in the form prescribed by the Secretary of the Treasury, or by law, that any articles in the list of imports are produced abroad by labor for which wages are paid equivalent to the wages paid in the United States of America for similar labor, these articles shall only pay a rate of import duty, say, twenty-five per cent. less than the regular rate of import duty charged upon such articles in said tariff." Such a proviso, which could be improved by a sliding scale of duties, rising with low wages, and falling with high wages, paid abroad on the production of the imported goods, would tend to produce among nations that equalization of fair wages, and reciprocity of beneficial commerce, which are the conditions of rational free trade.

The undenominational general representative assembly, or legislature, of the republic, or integral organ, of industry—for a state or nation—must consist of representatives chosen by the intermediate undenominational associations indiscriminately from all the general industrial classes.

It may enact general industrial regulations, which may be called general industrial positive laws, or public industrial contracts; appoint Executive Industrial Commissioners, for collecting and distributing useful industrial statistics; for awarding limited privileges, by letters patent, to inventors of useful industrial contrivances or combinations; for granting charters to incorporate industrial corporations; for exercising supervision and control over industrial corporations of a public nature, and for receiving and disbursing whatever revenue it may control.

There may be, for a state or a nation, a general denominational legislature of industry, consisting of two branches, elected at different times. Its members will be representatives, respectively, of the four fundamental industrial classes. As these classes are integral, and to some extent interpenetrate each other, and the class of consumers actually contains all the other classes, one branch of the denominational legislature may be composed exclusively of representatives of the consumers, and may be elected by the intermediate local associations convened to act undenominationally for all the classes of industry.

The other branch of the denominational legislature of industry may consist of an equal number of representatives, unless another proportion can be agreed on, for each of the other three industrial classes,—workingmen, employers, and capitalists,—and elected from the respective associations or corporations belonging to them. Perhaps the most practical way to elect separate representatives for these three classes, would be to let the elections be made by the regularly organized and combined associations of each class, respectively, say, by organized labor, by organized capital, and by the organized employers.

In this way, there would be assembled in both branches of the general denominational legislature of industry, an adequate number of recognized representatives of each fundamental industrial class; and their points of difference and points of agreement would be clearly brought out for rational deliberation by intelligent discussion.

The general denominational legislature of industry will settle by its resolutions the temporary general differences among the industrial classes; adjust a standard scale of wages and of hours of labor, as a practical basis for private contracts on the subject, while leaving all fair private contracts free; and appoint an advisory board to recommend temporary modifications of this scale, when they are required by changes of general economical circumstances.

It is probable that the discussions of the two branches of the general denominational industrial legislature, by demonstrating the truth of the principle, that in the long run, and in a large view, the interests of the four industrial classes are identical, would stop the industrial war now raging throughout the civilized world, and establish universal industrial peace.

It is not difficult to prove that it is the true interest of the consumer to pay a fair price for a good article; for this price will return to the consumer, who is a working-man, fair wages, and it will leave to the consumer, who is an employer, a fair profit; and it will yield to the consumer, who is a capitalist, a fair rate of interest. Again, fair wages, with a due regard to the hours of labor, are plainly the highest that can be paid consistently with the security and maintenance of capital, and it is as clearly the true interest of the working-men, with a view to preserving the source of wages, to receive no more, as it is the true policy of employers and capitalists, in order to keep up the consuming power of the working-men, from whom a large part of their profits is derived, to pay no less.

The republic, or integral organ, of industry, therefore, in its normal action, is a unity, an integral whole of action; the true permanent interests of all its members, its consumers, employers, working-men, and capitalists, in a system of intelligent harmony, and rationally organized industrial peace, being virtually the same.

ARTICLE V.

62. The Republic, or Integral Organ, of Public Charity.

The elementary activity of the republic, or integral organ, of public charity, is the public-spirited helping love of the people. It aims to remedy the deficiency of the action of each of the other four integral organs of society, and also to cure the evils common to them all.

Its means, besides its own action, are charitable gifts entrusted to it.

Its action, being public, is effected by associations, some of which are local, and others are confined to no locality. Hence, to accomplish its general aims, there have been developed in it five general groups or classes of charitable and benevolent associations.

One group of charitable associations supplements the general action of the republic of letters and art, by extending the benefits of education to the decrepit, the idiotic, the deaf and dumb, the blind, the incurably sick, whom the general system of public education does not effectually reach.

Another group of charitable associations ekes out the general action of the church by extending the benefits of its religious service to persons to whom the ordinary ministrations of the church do not extend,—the sick, the prisoner, the outcast, the dweller in thinly settled neighborhoods, the heathen.

Another group of charitable associations aids the deficencies in the ordinary working of the republic of industry; alleviates by generous contributions the calamities of bad harvests, of floods, of fires, of disappointments to the industrious poor, caused by unforeseen changes of trade, and by new applications of machinery; and seeks to protect working-men, working-women, and working children from excessive hours and unwholesome conditions of labor, and from labor at too early an age; and to preserve for them every week a day, and somewhat more, of rest.

Another group of charitable associations superadds its action to the government's dealing with crime; aids in deserving cases the defense of the accused, counsels with humanity the condemned, seeks to convert their punishment into means for their reform, and, after the term of their punishment expires, leads them with generous sympathy and needed assistance into honest courses of life.

The remaining group of charitable associations relieves the infirmities of immorality common, more or less, to all the integral organs, by promoting moral reforms; humanizes, refines, and elevates the modes of intercourse among the individuals and the collective members of society, by providing cheap, æsthetic public entertainments of high art.

The undenominational general representative assembly, or legislature, of the republic, or integral organ, of public charity, must consist of representatives chosen by the intermediate undenominational associations, convened to consider the general interests of public charity.

Its duty will be to collect and distribute statistics of public charity; to issue general advisory regulations on the subject, and to appoint a board of Executive Commissioners of Public Charity.

The duties of the executive commissioners of public charity would be, to examine and report, from time to time, the condition of all permanent charitable investments; to furnish practicable plans for all extensive charitable enterprises, when required by those having them in charge; and to make, under the direction of the associations engaged in the promotion of moral reforms, and of refined social intercourse, all the necessary arrangements for cheap, æsthetic public entertainments or amusements, by means of literary lectures, and of displays of high art in theatrical performances, and in other exhibitions, easily accessible to the masses of the people.

The denominational general representative assembly, or legislature, of the republic, or integral organ, of public charity, must be composed of representatives, elected as far as possible from all the general groups, orders or classes of charitable associations, and associations specially designed to promote moral reforms.

Its duty will be to harmonize by its deliberations the action of the various groups of associations engaged in charitable and reformatory work; and to furnish statistics and suggestions for general regulations to the undenominational legislature of the republic, or integral organ, of public charity.

Evidently, there may be an international and an Interrace organization of public charity, as well as of the other integral organs of society.

But charity, being as universal, and as ever present, as humanity, need not wait for the formation of international or Interrace charitable associations, in order to extend its help from one nation to another nation of the same or of another race. A national association, therefore, of the white race, in the United States of America, can properly perform an act of Interrace charity by assisting with money and counsel the negro nation sojourning there to emigrate to its natural habitat and providential home in Central Africa.

Similarly, acts of Interrace charity, though of a different kind, are performed by national associations of the white race in the United States of America to the Indian race now there.

In its normal action, the republic, or integral *organ* of public charity, is a unity, or integral whole of action, supplementing and rounding up the action of all the other integral organs, with itself, into a consistent whole, by its public-spirited helping love.

ARTICLE VI.

63. The Republic, or Integral Organ, of Government.

The elementary activity of the republic, or integral organ of government, is to defend and secure the public peace, to preserve domestic tranquillity and harmony, to prevent and detect crime, to punish criminals, and to administer the law in litigated cases.

Its means are the wealth of the nation levied by taxation; the physical force of the nation organized as a police, militia and navy; the enactment of general governmental positive laws, and the establishment of courts of justice.

The modes of action of the elementary activity of government, may be gathered into four groups, represented by the action of the four partial organs of government, which are: its Political Parties, its Governmental Legislature, its body of Executive officers, and its Legal Profession, divided into an Official or Judicial branch, and a Lay, or practicing branch.

The limited sphere of the modes of action of the government, as indicated by the above enumeration of its partial organs, will be best understood by considering that the government, which in the system of ancient heathenism, or Orientalism, now superseded by Christianity, contained all the functions of society, has been gradually emptied of the functions properly belonging to the republic of letters and art, to the republic of the church, to the republic of industry, and to the republic of public charity; and that it now retains only the functions strictly pertaining to normal government.

The progress heretofore made in divesting the government of the functions which, in its ancient heathen or Oriental form, it had usurped from the other integral organs of society, leads to the inference that the government, even as now constituted, will be considered in the future as either the needless duplicate, or the non-essential auxiliary of the other integral organs; either arbitrarily taking up the functions which they voluntarily or by force abandon, or discretionally aiding functions which they inefficiently exercise. Hence, it seems probable, that if the other integral organs will act intelligently and energetically in discharging their proper functions, the government will be still further simplified.

Indeed, when, by systematic public education, the republic of letters and art endows the community with liberal culture in the principles of physical, moral, religious and æsthetic science; when the republic of the church exercises the people in true religious service, that leads them to imitate God's true character; when the republic of industry conducts its industrial affairs on a system of wise and equitable principles, doing exact justice to every industrial class; and when the republic of public charity refines and humanizes the masses of men in their intercourse with each other, and ennobles them by moral reforms, it is evident that nothing will remain for the government to do.

It is true that, owing to the unconscious color-blindness of the reforming as well as of the conservative chiefs of society, preventing them from recognizing and following the one faithfully leading light of the world, to the Kingdom of God, society may never on earth arrive at this ideal condition; but that it may approximate it here, with a continued simplification of the government, is not an irrational supposition. The mere practical adoption of industrial principles, that would stay the present universal industrial war; and of legal principles that would abolish the present system of offensive and conquering political war; to say nothing of a general, rational, religious reformation, would be a long step towards this desirable consummation.

The nature, the duties, and the organization, respectively, of the partial organs of the integral organ of government, will now be briefly stated.

64. The government's Political Parties, as distinguished from factions, or rings, and from the supporters of rings, are honorable associations of independent voters, acting with deliberate, instinctive thought, on all available information, and with the observance of all pertinent principles, for the practical determination of the current governmental questions of the day. They deserve a place in the written constitution of every state and nation.

Each political party acts collectively by nominating and voting for representatives of its party for the ordinary governmental legislature, and also for the leading executive officers of the government. The political parties together constitute the whole people, and each professes to act for the general welfare. They differ, not on principles, because these are common to all the people; but on practical measures, involving the application of these principles.

The organization of each political party is formed by assembling in central points in the intermediate districts, respectively, representatives from primary local meetings of its members in each of the primary territorial districts, and so on. The representative meetings of each political party nominate its candidates for the ordinary governmental legislature, and for the leading executive officers of the government; and the members of the party afterwards vote for these candidates in the general elections of the people.

Political parties are sometimes local, and sometimes general, or national, according to the scope of the issues or questions which they maintain. Individuals belonging to the same party on national questions, may belong to different parties on municipal questions.

The proper organization of political parties requires the erection in each primary district, or neighborhood, of neighborhood houses, with central houses in the intermediate districts, and in central points of each state or nation, arranged with a convenient number of apartments; so that the members of each party may meet separately, either on the same or on different days, to become acquainted, and to consult with each other on public questions. And there may be a room where all parties, if they choose, may meet together.

These neighborhood houses, and the central houses connected with them, may be so arranged as to accommodate, for some purposes, by courtesy, all the integral organs; and the accommodations they require will suggest a new order of public · architecture. But, as they would be primarily intended to promote the proper action of political parties, they should be constructed by the national and local governments.

By this arrangement for friendly and frequent consultation, the masses of each political party may become personally known to each other in the primary districts, and come to the general election well informed as to all political questions and political movements, and well prepared, without dictation from any ring, and without undue influence from any quarter, to vote upon them understandingly. In this way may be secured, for every political party, the advantages which the local Demes, introduced by Clisthenes into Athens, gave to the Athenian democracy in its most glorious days.

An important precaution to secure spontaneity of action and free deliberation in the nomination of candidates for election, would be to require all ballots or tickets voted for this purpose in the primary meetings of political parties, as well as in nominating conventions, to be written by those who cast them.

Old political parties will be dissolved, and new parties formed, as old practical questions are settled, and new practical questions arise; thus keeping up a healthy current of popular political life, in changing practical political parties, according to the practical exigencies of the times, while the same fundamental principles, held by them all, live on forever. For a political party can no more have peculiar principles to act by, than it can have peculiar sunshine to bask in, or peculiar air to breathe.

Political parties should pay their own necessary expenses, by a small voluntary contribution from each member, as does every other honorable association that pursues an object of common interest to all its members. To preserve equality among their members, they should not allow the payment of any contribution above a low measure, to be fixed from time to time, say one dollar from any one person.

Hence, a political party, as an honorable association of equal members, cannot tax its candidates, or the holders or expectants of public offices, higher than its other members. For a higher tax implies that the public offices are not primarily held for the benefit of the public, but of a ring, by whom the tax is impudently imposed, or more impudently assumed, as an investment to be repaid, with profit, by public offices or jobs.

65. The government's regular, or denominational legislature consists of representatives elected, in fact, by the people in general, but virtually delegated by the political parties by whom they were nominated. Its sphere, according to the territory it represents, will be national or local.

Its action should be confined to what is strictly governmental. Its business should be divided into two classes: one class, being temporary matters of governmental business, relating chiefly to the taxes, their disbursement, and necessary loans; the other class, being general governmental positive laws. The first class should chiefly occupy the legislature's time. The other class, the general positive laws, should only receive additions or amendments at long intervals, and only when demanded by urgent necessity, after full deliberation, to keep pace with the development of principles.

The organization of the legislature should be either in two co-ordinate bodies elected for different terms, or in one body with members elected for different terms; so that at every session it would receive new members, to succeed those whose terms had expired. It should have the usual standing committees, and such special committees, and joint conference committees, as its business demands. It should also adopt for its guidance parliamentary rules, framed to secure the deliberate dispatch of business. Its sessions should be frequent, and if annual, should be short.

Its enactments should require the concurrence of the chief executive officer of the territorial sphere, or locality represented by it, if he is elected by the people; but they could be passed, notwithstanding his objections, by the votes of two-thirds of the legislature, if it is one body; or of each of its bodies, if it is composed of two branches.

It is proper, also, that the concurrence of the legislature, or of one branch of it, should be required to ratify some special action of the chief executive officer, co-ordinate with it, such as, in general, the appointment of a few executive and judicial officers; or in regard to the action of the chief executive officer of a nation, in the conclusion of treaties with foreign nations.

Besides the general governmental legislature of a nation, there will be corresponding subordinate legislatures for each of its states or provinces, and further subordinate legislatures for its municipalities, and its intermediate districts; each of these legislatures being limited in its sphere of action to the governmental interests exclusively affecting the locality it represents.

International, or even Interrace, governmental legislatures, if, in the distant future, they should come to be required, could be easily organized, according to the principles of civil representative democracy, and of international and Interrace law.

66. The body of Executive officers of a national government should consist of a chief executive, or president, elected by the whole people, and of different grades of subordinate executive officers, appointed directly or indirectly by him, both for the civil and for the military service, including the army and navy.

Corresponding also to the series of subordinate governmental legislatures, for states, provinces, municipalities, and intermediate districts, there are sets of chief and subordinate executive officers, respectively, for each legislature; but, as they are in many respects analogous to the set belonging to the general government of a nation, nothing further need here be said of them, except that the local chief executive officers mainly control the local police; while the chief executive officer of the nation commands the national militia and the navy.

Besides the chief executive officer of the national government, there must be, under him, for the civil service two principal classes of subordinate executive officers; one class being leading executive officers, the other class being ministerial executive officers.

Of the military and naval service it is only necessary to say that it is subject to the ordinary military rules, and is subordinate to the civil power.

The duties of the whole body of the executive officers of the civil service of the nation are as follows: It is the duty of the chief executive officer to superintend generally the execution of the leading measures of the government as devised by the legislature and prescribed by the laws; it is the duty of the leading subordinate executive officers to plan and practically direct, under the supervision of their chief, the execution of these measures; and it is the duty of the ministerial subordinate class of executive officers, to specifically execute the details of these measures under the orders of the leading class.

Then, among the class of ministerial subordinate executive officers, who in a populous nation must be very numerous, there must be a few confidential officers, known to the leading officers, and trusted by them, to have general charge, as chiefs of bureaus, or foremen, over particular spheres of executive work.

The chief executive officer must be directly responsible for his immediate subordinates, the leading subordinate executive officers; one of whom should be the legal counsellor of the executive branch of the government, while the others are the heads of the various other executive departments; and they should each, respectively, be directly responsible for the ministerial executive officers subordinate to them, especially for those designated as confidential. The chief executive officer, therefore, should appoint the leading subordinate executive officers; but he may be required to report their names for confirmation to the legislature, or one branch of it; and the legislative body to whom they are reported shall be considered as confirming them, unless it objects to them by a two-thirds vote, within a week from his report. The leading executive officer at the head of each department, shall appoint the confidential ministerial officers belonging to his department, subject to the approval of the chief executive officer.

The remaining mass of subordinate ministerial executive officers below the confidential class, should be regarded as a standing body of public servants, like the privates and lower officers of the army and navy. They should be so organized, and the affairs of the government should be so simplified, by discarding from it all matters not strictly governmental—as, for instance, the post-office, which is the proper business of an express company—that their number could be reduced to the actual wants of the government; and their compensation should be made equal to that paid in private life for such services as they perform.

They should be appointed only after a successful examination, and their removal should be made only by the head of their department, and for inefficiency, negligence, or misconduct only.

Any vacancy among them should be filled, from the number of qualified applicants, by the head of the department in which it occurs.

A proper commission should conduct the examination of applicants, and report it, with their age, which, if mature, should not alone exclude them; and the same commission should hear appeals from those who are removed. But an appeal from the decision of the commission may be taken to the chief executive officer by the head of the department making the removal.

In this way the influence of political parties will be confined to its legitimate sphere, the chief executive office, the leading subordinate executive offices, and the confidential subordinate ministerial executive offices. Otherwise there is an obvious danger that, if political parties allow their respective organizations to enter into a rivalry with each other, to obtain the numerous minor offices of the government, and if they give a license to the rapacity of their officious, brawling partisans to claim them as rewards for pretended services to their party, rewards won by them either as spoils of a meretricious victory, or as prizes in a game of trickery and fraud, political parties will be degraded from honorable associations, inspired by generous, patriotic principles, into dishonorable, selfish factions.

67. The Legal Profession is a voluntary association, the admission to which is regulated by law, subject to a prescribed examination as to the professional or legal knowledge, and the moral character, of the applicant. It is divided into two branches; the official or judicial branch, and the lay or practicing branch. Its object is to render service in the administration of justice.

The official or judicial branch are the judges of the courts, and the official legal advisers and representatives of the government, taken from the lay or practicing branch. The lay or practicing branch is composed of the rest of the legal profession.

The duty of the courts, as the judicial branch of the legal profession, or the judicial department of the government, is to decide litigated cases according to the law; with the help, in criminal cases, of a legal prosecutor representing the government, in fairness, and of a practicing lawyer representing the accused, in just defense; and with the aid, in civil cases, of practicing lawyers, on both sides.

The duty of both branches of the legal profession is to maintain, in their expressed opinions, and in all their other legal acts, the supremacy of the law. To this end they should study law as a science, based on the philosophy of law, and elucidated by modern historical researches into the remotest antiquity; and should discard the heathen and despotic maxims and precedents that

have come down to the present day, in the current doctrine of the legal profession, from the ancient heathenism and Orientalism that preceded Christianity.

If the law is viewed as a science based on true philosophy, it will rest on the Semitic philosophy, which
deduces all principles from the First Principle, and this
from the uniform action of God; the rules or uniformities of which, in its morality and justice, man is bound,
by the original and continuing social contract of God
with man, to imitate as derivative principles of law,
regulating the conduct of man to man. Hence, all the
principles of law, being derived, like all the so-called
Christian laws of nature, from the First Principle, and
being consequently not made by man but by God, are
a higher law, paramount over all positive law, all of
which is of human origin.

There was a remarkable anticipation of this higher
law, though in somewhat confused and imperfect state-
ments, by the great jurists of the ancient Roman law.
They, too, treated law as a science, and based it on
philosophy; but the foundation on which they placed
it was the heathen philosophy of the Stoics. Among
their legal maxims, or rules of law, they distinguished
some as rational from others as positive; deriving the
former from their philosophy, calling them separately
laws of nature, or collectively natural law, and regarding
them as "laws of laws;" thus reaching in their speculative theory, the logical conclusion, which in their
despotic government they dared not practically apply,
or even openly avow,—that their rational rules of law,
as "laws of laws," or what we call the principles of law,

were of higher authority than all positive laws. But the great truth, that principle is a higher law than positive law, was practically vindicated, to a great extent, by the ancient Roman Prætorian law, which was the law introduced by the decisions of the Roman Prætors; who, in their official public edicts, upon entering on their office,—relying upon the public conscience, the public intelligence, and the general support of the legal profession,—boldly proclaimed the legal rules by which their decisions would be guided; thus laying down, from time to time, rational rules, or "laws of laws," derived from their philosophy and their law of nature, whereby gradually many of the barbaric "positive rules" of the old Roman law were superseded.

But, it must not be forgotten, that the philosophical legal system of ancient Rome, however relatively admirable when compared with other ancient bodies of law, is the scheme of heathen Stoic philosophy, and that the law of nature referred to in ancient Roman jurisprudence is a heathen law of nature, the law by which that philosophy imagined that Zeus, the immoral chief Roman idol divinity, governed his mythical "City of Zeus." Now, the heathen natural law contains many gross abominations, such as license to wage offensive war and to make conquests, and is altogether different from the Christian law of nature, as the law of God, or the principle of law. Hence, although it was a memorable event, for his day and generation, when the Dutch lawyer, Grotius, set up, in imagination, his curule chair, like a Roman Prætor, assuming to judge among the nations of the civilized world, as if they were simple

Roman proprietors, and when assuming the moral authority of that magistrate, while sustained by the unanimous voice of the public, he issued his prætorian edict, as it were, in his treatise, "On the Law of War and of Peace," requiring them to demean themselves towards each other according to the rules of the Roman natural law; yet, the present day demands the proclamation of a more ancient and a higher law,—the very law of principle and of God. This law forbids offensive war and conquest, and requires the nations to unite their rational efforts for the general welfare.

Among the legal maxims, still current in law books, and descended from the system of ancient heathenism and Orientalism, is the maxim that positive law is the "command of a political superior." But in the normal form of government, in civil representative democracy, there is no political superior; and all positive laws are public contracts, made by and among the people, either immediately and tacitly among themselves, and evidenced by custom; or mediately and expressly, by their duly authorized agents, assembled in a legislature, or in a diplomatic meeting. Positive laws, therefore, must, like all contracts, be conformed to and controlled by principle.

It will be the duty of the legal profession to frame a code of common positive law consistent with principle, and fit for universal adoption.

It is also manifest that positive laws, when made among the nations of the same race, whether immediately or by agents, will be international; and when made in either of these modes, among different races, will be Interrace.

All grave questions of domestic or foreign governmental policy can be put into the form of a public contract, either as the subject matter of a statute, or of a treaty. They must all involve a question of law, and the same test, by principle, as to the legal validity of such a contract, will apply to the question of its expediency; both questions resting on the same ultimate grounds. For, as the law is conceded, as principle, or as the law of God, to be the perfection of reason, the question, What is the rule of law resulting from the facts, or from a proposed contract, in a particular case? and the question, What is expedient, in the light of the highest reason, under all circumstances of that case? are virtually identical. Hence, it is the duty of the legal profession to mature and express, for the guidance of the public, deliberate opinions on the legal bearings of all important public measures; and, in order to enable them to do so, by earnestly cultivating the study, and by jointly asserting the paramount authority, of principle, they should perfect their organization.

When, as the prophet predicted, the knowledge of God shall cover the earth as the water covereth the sea, the knowledge of the law will become universal. Then, in the ultimate simplification of the government, the legal profession, as is already indicated by the phenomenal increase of its numbers, will be absorbed into the general community. But, until that period arrives, the importance of organizing the legal profession, and of thereby aiding its mission to maintain the present authority of principle, and thus to secure the progress of society without forcible revolutions, should not be overlooked.

The legal profession should be organized as a voluntary association, or general guild, for joint deliberation and council, aiming to secure its own and the public advantage, by promoting the liberal culture and the moral conduct of its members in both its branches. It should pursue the usual mode of undenominational representative organization, by convening in a central or convenient place in each nation, state or province, representatives chosen indiscriminately from all its classes by primary local meetings of its members in the intermediate territorial districts of the nation, state, or province; a nation composed of only one state having only one representative meeting; and a nation composed of several states or provinces having a representative meeting for each of them, and also a central national representative meeting of delegates from each of the state or provincial meetings. An international representative meeting would consist of delegates chosen by the national meetings. An Interrace representative meeting could be chosen by the several international meetings. The lower representative meetings, in their choice of delegates to the higher representative meetings, should not be confined to their own members. The terms of all representatives should be short, and shorter for the lower than for the higher meetings; and all representatives should be re-eligible. A national representative meeting,. or convention, of the legal profession should appoint the days and places of its elections and meetings, and the terms of its representatives and delegates. Care should be taken that, in the primary meetings of the profession, of which due notice should be given, every member of every class should be free to participate; and should thus share in all the benefits, and be bound by all the constraints, of the whole organization. In this way, professional rings and close corporations of the few would be avoided, with their partial views; and the whole legal profession, after freeing itself of those who do not legally or properly belong to it, would be raised to a higher and more liberal standard, both of excellence and of influence.

The judges, the prosecuting officers, and the sheriffs, or higher executive officers connected with the courts of the state, province, or nation, should be elected for a permanent term, from the legal profession, by a plurality vote of the people, without reference to political parties. The judges should appoint the other officers of their courts.

The courts should not be unnecessarily numerous; but should form a system, each being complete, with a judge, or a bench of judges, to decide questions of law; a jury, to ascertain matters of fact; a recording officer, to record its proceedings, and bailiffs, or executive officers, to execute its processes. Some should have original, and others appellate jurisdiction, in order to afford an opportunity, in the interest of justice, to correct any errors committed in the first hearing of a case. The lowest courts, for small cases, should have as able judges as the highest.

But, where principle is held to be paramount over positive law, and to control all contracts, there cannot be a separate set of equity courts.

The officers of the courts should receive moderate and regular salaries; and the costs of the courts should be so regulated as to relieve the suitors of the courts from unnecessary burdens, and should not be paid to their officers. For, in courts having much business, the fees paid to their officers by the suitors constitute emoluments so extravagant as to make the positions of these officers coveted prizes in the eyes of political factions, and to exert a corrupting influence on the election of the judges; especially where judges and the officers of their courts are elected by political parties, and are nominated in the same party convention.

68. The four partial organs of the government, its political parties, its ordinary or denominational governmental legislature, its body of executive officers, and its legal profession, with its official or judicial branch, and its lay or practicing branch, having been sufficiently discussed, there only remains to be considered its extraordinary or Undenominational General Representative Assembly, called its general governmental convention, for exercising the people's reserved powers, whether legislative, executive, or judicial, as required by the occasion. It is a well known and effective agency of the government, often employed in modern times, to change the form of government, or to remove dangerous or otherwise objectionable persons from public office, with the consent of the people. It effects, in a peaceable way, without any disturbance of public order, the same

results that could only otherwise be accomplished by a violent revolution or civil war.

Its application presupposes that the people are sufficiently informed and instructed to note, from time to time, the emergence of principles, which are not merely opposed to positive laws of long standing and of high authority, but which also herald, by that opposition, the advent of great political reforms and- revolutions. The effectual assertion of a great political principle in opposition to ancient positive law, is a successful revolution; and it may be accomplished as thoroughly by the resolution of a convention as by a revolutionary uprising of the people.

The undenominational general representative assembly, or convention, of the integral organ of government, its highest legislature, may be of a nation or of a state, if the nation contains more than one state; and it consists of representatives from the intermediate districts of the nation or state, chosen from the people indiscriminately, without regard to the partial organs of the government.

It is called together by the express or implied general agreement of the people; and is invested with all their power, so far as necessary to effect the purposes for which it is called. It is only brought into existence, upon rare occasions, to formally inaugurate great political reforms, which have already virtually been decided upon, or admitted to be necessary by the people.

It exercises the reserved powers of the people; and it is able, therefore, not only to modify the present institutions or elements of the government, but also, when a suitable occasion arises, to add to them. For instance, in addition to the present courts, and above them, it could establish a Political Tribunal, with jurisdiction to try and punish for official misconduct, whether political or moral, the highest legislative, executive and judicial officers of the government, as well as other persons; and especially all persons guilty of high crimes against the majesty or sovereignty of the people.

The whole republic, or integral organ, of government, in its normal action, as a civil representative democracy, will exhibit, on a review of all its functions, a unity, or integral whole, of action. For while its political parties are enlightened and honorable associations, agreeing upon all fundamental principles, and differing only in practical measures; and its legislature is virtually composed of conference committees delegated from its political parties, and deliberately advising with each other, settling their party differences in regard to these practical measures, by public contracts of the whole people, in the form of positive laws; and its executive officers see to the maintenance of public order and the due execution of the laws; its legal profession, by the co-operation of both its branches, in one united organization, will not only urge the reduction of all positive laws, man's imperfect inventions, to a harmonious system, by requiring their conformity to God's paramount universal principles, but it will also inaugurate, in the correct decision of litigated cases, according to the rule of principle, the universal reign of absolute justice.

Such, as has been sketched, being the normal Social Constitution of mankind, already approximated in the modern civilization of the white race, and serving as an example to the other races, it is manifest that Law, the higher law of God, the uniformity of the uniformities of God's action, or the First Principle of the Semitic philosophy, as in nature, so in mind and in society, or in the whole Kingdom of God, is the predominant, the ruling, and the harmonizing power.

CHAPTER V.

THE General Social Reformation, as the revived, predominantly practical side, of the Semitic Philosophy, and called Practical Christianity, or developed Modern Civilization, is attainable by all monotheistic nations and races.

69. The Semitic philosophy, as we have traced it, is an exposition, or a general explanatory and descriptive view of the Kingdom of God, as a reality, as the one universal fact, which, although it cannot be fully expressed, and can only be indicated, by language, can, by means of the instinctive ideas, be clearly conceived and rationally developed by instinctive thought. The Semitic philosophy explains the nature, and describes the prevailing order of the Kingdom of God, as the universe.

It explains the nature of it as being, in part, spiritual, composed of one superior spirit, God, of the spirits of mankind, and the spirits of the inferior animals and plants; and in part material, consisting of matter; distinguishing spirit from matter by their respective qualities, and showing that the qualities of the one are absolutely, and in all respects, different from those of the other.

It describes the order prevailing in the universe, as the uniformity of the uniformities of God's action, and as such the one First Principle, at once speculative and practical, from which all others are derived, and as potentially consisting of two derivative systems of principles; one system being rules for the actions of the spiritual part of the universe, and the other system being rules for the motions of its material part; and both systems comprising the laws of God, which are sometimes erroneously called, from a dogma of the heathen Stoic philosophy, the laws of nature.

70. It then uses the relation of man's spirit to his body,—a relation analogous, in some respects, to that of the spirits of lower animals and plants, respectively, to their bodies,—to explain in other respects the relation of God, as the one superior spirit, to the whole inorganic world, or material universe; and, after proving by the intuitive evidence of consciousness, in voluntarily raising an arm, that man's spirit, by its immediate practical action, causes within the body to which it is confined original motion in matter, it infers that all original motion of matter is caused by the immediate practical action of spirit; the original motions of the organic world by the immediate action of the spirits inhabiting, respectively, its several parts, as their bodies; and the original motions of the whole inorganic world, or the material universe, outside of their bodies, by the immediate action of God.

Hence, it follows that both the systems of rules, or laws, for actions of spirit and for original motions of matter, respectively, are primarily laws for the normal action of spirit; and that the one First Principle, comprising both systems, and being the uniformity of the uniformi-

tics of God's action, takes in the uniformities, or laws of
man's normal action; man being the image, and his
normal action being the imitation, of God.

71. The Kingdom of God, abstractly regarded, is the
First Principle, which is related to the derivative principles, or laws, of all the speculative and practical, physical
and natural sciences, either as the root to the ramifica-
tions of a tree, or as a river to the branches contributing
by their inflow to its volume; according as, in one view,
the unity of the one God as their immediate origin, or, in
the other view, the variety of his operations in them,
is chiefly noticed; although likewise, even when the First
Principle is likened to a river with numerous tributaries,
themselves receiving the supply of many springs, and
these replenished from the lofty and swiftly moving
clouds, it has then, too, in the spirit of God, as the
river in the bosom of the ocean, one ultimate source.

The Kingdom of God, concretely conceived, is the
compound system of the spiritual and the material universe ; including in its spiritual element God and man
related to each other as the society of God and man,
related also to the organic world outside of man, and to
the inorganic world; and including likewise, as its material element, that inorganic world as the instrument and
the passive means used by the spiritual universe for realizing its action.

The concrete Kingdom of God exhibits the effects of
God's action, through the First Principle, upon the
universe. In this way, he acts immediately, directly,
constantly, and with uniformity, upon the material universe outside of the organic world, that is, upon the

inorganic world, by imparting to it original molecular and relative motions, the combinations of which determine in matter its various qualities and relations. Of these it is only necessary here to say that all the problems of physical science are now found to be questions of motion.

Further, in the concrete Kingdom of God, by the same First Principle, God acts mediately, and indirectly upon the spiritual universe, and especially upon the spirit of man; using matter as the means of communicating both his speculative and his practical action. Thus he foreshadows, by useful modifications of matter, adapted to man's recurring necessities, the elementary practical activities of man, and with them the social contract of God with man, and the resulting normal organization of society. This is easily proved.

For matter is evidently a necessary medium for communicating the action of spirit from spirit to spirit. The form of matter, viewed as a medium for communicating the spirit's speculative action, is a sign; and viewed as a medium for communicating the spirit's practical action, it is a tool or instrument.

Matter is also used to preserve and store, for future use, both the speculative and the practical action imparted to it by man; speculative action, in books and monuments; practical action, in provisions of food, and in money. Similarly, it is recorded that in ancient days, as now, signs of the times indicating God's thoughts and purposes, have been always recognized by man in the changing forms of the inorganic world, whether in the inspiring succession of the seasons, or in the expressive

face of the heavens; and it is manifest from the researches of modern science, that the earth, the sun, and
the stellar universe are not only eternal monuments of
God's wisdom for the instruction, but also stores of
correlated various energy for the practical use, of man
and all the spiritual universe.

72. The action of spirit being integral, its speculative
and its practical action are simultaneous and interfused;
its practical action shaping matter, both as a conductor
to convey integral spiritual action, and as a sign to express its speculative meaning. Thus, man's body, as
we have seen, is a complicated instrument, framed by
his spirit, for transmitting the integral spiritual action
reflected from outward objects to its inward parts, supposed to be the brain, constituting the material sensuous
ideas, and for enabling that action to inscribe them as
signs of the speculative meaning it is designed to convey.

It is through his body, therefore, that man, apart
from the spiritual action he receives from his fellow-
man and the rest of the organic world, takes in the
spiritual action of the superior spirit, God, reflected from
the inorganic world; and it is by the interpretation of
the sensuous ideas, as signs of that action, that he learns
its intention and design to be the loving service of God
to all mankind.

That service man, by reflection, comes to know as
consisting of the First Principle, and God's resulting
elementary practical activities of instruction, religious
service, or communion, industry, charity, and government; the imitation and pursuit of which activities,
again, by man, leads him, he sees, into the association

of God with man, or the original social contract. For the isolated individual is impelled, by the conscious similarity and inferiority of his spiritual nature to that of God, to accept the instruction of the superior spirit, and, in pursuance of it, to imitate the other practical activities of God, and thus to work with him. Further, when man observes the presence of other spiritual beings similar and equal to himself, and working, like himself, with God, he groups and associates himself with them, as a class of equals, working together, for the benefit of each other, under the one common superior spirit, and he infers that all the elementary activities of God are designed both for the imitation and for the benefit of all men alike, and are intended to bring about their universal co-operation.

73. Then follows the conviction of every man, that if he would imitate God, he must serve all men, and serve them, as he is served, by means of those elementary activities. The result is a normal association of all men with each other, for their common benefit under God. This is at first an undenominational association, giving equal attention to all the elementary activities. Afterwards, as the operations of the original association become extended, it is ideally divided into denominational associations, or integral organs, for each of the elementary activities. The original and the denominational associations, with their individuals, while normal, and properly doing their own work, are helping each other, and are also, in this way, doing the work of God. Thus God and mankind are working together, are associated

This association of God with man, is the original and continuing social contract. In its formation language has no place, but is represented by the sensuous ideas. It is a contract by action, without words. It is continuing, perpetual, and potentially universal. It embraces all on whose hearts the law of God is written, or who have a knowledge of the true character of God; but those who, from ignorance, fail to enter into this covenant with God, are not therefore excluded from his providential care. The domain of the social contract is extended by the positive law, which rests on it, and includes it as also the First Principle, and all other principles with the first, and which binds all who enter society and enjoy its benefits, whether they have a particular knowledge of the social contract or not.

Like all valid contracts, the social contract has a consideration on both sides. The consideration on man's part is his recognition of the universality of the contract, and his consequent implied engagement that man shall not selfishly attempt to monopolize the aid God gives to all men in his principles and laws; but shall altruistically assist God in blessing all other men; and the consideration on God's part is, that he will continue his principles or laws unchanged, for man's present benefit and for his future reliance.

From the social contract is derived, as we have seen, the normal organization of society, with its five integral organs.

74. Each of the five integral organs, in its normal action, and all, as comprising together the whole social organization, have been described; and there only remains

the task to point out in each of them some of the errors and irregularities that hinder its normal action, and prevent its full development. On these errors there will first be given some general remarks, to show their united scope; afterwards a few of the most important will be discussed in view of their removal by a general reformation of society.

In the republic of letters and art, if the views before advanced in these papers are admitted, some false science, so called, is left for future correction, in the extravagances of evolution, of agnosticism, of monism, idealism, and materialism. But the correction of these errors, after what has been said, may be confidently left to the zealous pursuit of truth in true science, which now universally engages the learned. As a consequence of this activity of the republic of letters and art, leading to a more general liberal culture, there must also ensue in the community a sound public opinion, a lively public conscience, and some general common sense, to guide and check the conduct of the mass of individuals.

In the republic of the church, not to reiterate questions of principle already discussed, it may be mentioned that its sacerdotal or governmental organization, after the model of a human government, is a very ancient abnormal institution, which is already eighteen centuries old in its present form, and is copied after a still more ancient heathen sacerdotal institution, reaching back thousands of years into earlier antiquity; but concerning this subject little more need be said, as the institution is suffering from the common ills of effete decay, to which all antiquated abnormal institutions, under the stress of inquiring reason, at last succumb.

In the republic of industry a universal industrial war has raged for many years, owing to abnormal industrial organization. Labor, under the social contract, is entitled to the equal benefit of the laws of God, both in the First Principle, and in their practical application. The ill-judged attempt of the employer and capitalist classes to monopolize the benefit of these laws, otherwise called the laws of nature, by securing for themselves exclusively the advantages of mechanical inventions and scientific discoveries, without according a corresponding increase of wages or decrease of the working hours, is the real source of grievance of the labor class; and the proper remedy will be the abandonment of violent methods and the resort to reason, by the labor class, and a rational appeal, in a normal industrial organization, to the consumer class, which controls, as it includes, all the industrial classes; as it has been demonstrated that the vital and lasting interests of all the industrial classes, in the matter of wages, as in all other important respects, are identical.

In the republic of public charity, devoted to the regulation of normal social intercourse, and to the promotion of public moral reforms, intoxication is encountered as a master public evil that requires the united energies of the people for its reformation.

In the republic of government, at home and abroad, there are many abuses calling for suitable remedies; but these abuses are not so universal as those of the other integral organs; government everywhere among the white race, except Russians, Poles, Turks, Arabians and Persians, having progressed far in the way from Oriental despotism to civil representative democracy. Yet all the partial organs of government need some reformation,— chiefly its political parties and its legal profession; as the reform of these two would include that of its legislature and its executive officers.

The disgraceful conduct of party leaders at home,— constituting a so-called ring, entirely distinct from, but within, each political party, which, as such, however, is an honorable association,—is illustrated by the action of such leaders, controlling the party, in accepting and counting notoriously fraudulent votes for their presidential candidate in 1876; again, in attempting to carry a presidential election by bribery; and, as charged, by accomplishing the election of a president by the same means. To charge such misdeeds on a political party would be a libel on popular government.

But the introducing of negro suffrage, in the country of the white race, is not the work of a ring, but of a party, by an error based on good intentions, and surely awaiting its correction from the people's "sober second thought."

The legal profession has furnished, notoriously, many members of the political rings of all parties; and it greatly needs a thorough, universal organization, to keep all its members under proper control, as well as to extend and confirm its legitimate and salutary influence.

75. A general reformation of society must be, from what has been said before, a more perfect realization of

the Kingdom of God, as an integral system of knowledge and of practice, both in the individual and in the community.

To be successful, it will require the co-operation of all genuine reformers in matters of education or science, of religion, of industry, of public charity, and of government. For these elementary activities form one integral social system, and any derangement in one of them obstructs the rest; so that every particular reform in one of them depends for its success on the general reform of all.

The harmonizing of the leaders of at least approximately all social reforms, the reform of the reformers, is a very great difficulty that must be encountered at the outset of a general social reformation. But, when once accomplished, it will produce a union and co-operation of forces that can be applied successively, with overpowering effect, to each of the needed reforms, and then eventually to make them all unite. At present, however, the advocates of one reform will strongly oppose another, while both can be shown to be necessary parts of one more general reform.

An embarrassment in the way of combined action for the reform of social errors and abuses, lies in the fact that some of them are both ancient and general; so that the attempt to reform them implies not only a criticism, the expression of which the discussion of the reform necessitates, on the past and present action of the great white race; but also a grave censure on our near ancestors, from whom we have inherited the institutions, good and evil, under which we live; and even on par-

ticular great men of the past, of whom we are justly
proud, but who are recorded in history as having originated, or at least supported, those evils. But, as
greatness and limitation are often found together in
the same race and in the same individual; to call
attention to the shortcoming of the truly great,
whether an individual or a race, and thereby to vindicate the truth of history, and to utilize its lessons for
the present and the future generations of mankind, is,
in fact, a necessary, although a reluctant, undertaking.

Now, when, in order to get a view of the general
social reformation that is demanded, we examine in
succession the present social errors and abuses, with
their remedies, we will find that these errors and abuses,
as departures in thought and practice from the one
First Principle, are intimately related to each other;
and that, for effecting their respective remedies as
partial revivals of that principle, in its various aspects,
a combined attempt to promote a general revival of
that principle, as the guiding element of the social contract, and as the necessary condition for realizing the
Kingdom of God, or perfect society, would suffice, and
would harmonize all the efforts necessary to bring about
that general social reformation.

The conception, in various stages of development, of
the First Principle, being common to all men, leading
them to expect, at the same time, the same series of
helpful or unfavorable events, and then jointly, to prepare for them, is the means by which the co-operation
of mankind in society is accomplished. For the past,
the present, and the future, as ultimate effects of the

uniform controlling action of God, being the continuous outward manifestation of that principle, the present containing the past as its cause, and the future as its effect; the conception of that principle enables man not only to explain the past by the present and the present by the past; but also by the past and the present to predict the future.

But, while a full and clear conception of the First ·Principle, as the uniformity of the uniformities of God's action, is of the highest importance for man's speculative and practical action, it can only be sought, and it must be gained, by careful observation and experiment, and the reasoned study of the resulting sensuous ideas, or so-called experience.

Such a clear conception of that principle, being a revival of it in man's consciousness, must be not only the source of the laws and predictions of all true science, but also the ground of that knowledge of the spiritual nature of God, of man, and of society, that is necessary to guide man in advancing and completing, by the normal organization of society, its general reformation.

But a scant, superficial, and careless conception of the First Principle, being a virtual departure from it, and involving a neglect of exact experience, with a resulting confusion of thought, must afford occasion, first, for self-deception and error concerning the material nature of the inorganic universe, and the laws of physical science; and then concerning the spiritual nature and action of God, of man and of society. The omission, therefore, of the leading integral organ of society, the republic of letters and art, to clearly conceive and appreciate the First Principle, must seriously obstruct a general social reformation.

76. Accordingly, the first of the fundamental errors. requiring a remedy in the general social reformation, and to be now examined, is the entertainment, even in the white race, by a great part of the republic of letters and art, of the false Oriental science handed down from the earliest historical times, and the consequent failure of that integral organ to fully apprehend the First Principle.

. That false, ancient Oriental science assigned a malignant moral character to matter, thereby making matter spiritual, and spirit consequently material. It thus confounded both, either as idealism or materialism, and culminated in idolatry; first, in Pantheism, which considers the whole material universe as God; and then in the subsequent multitudinous forms of idolatry, arising from splitting up the conception of the inorganic world as God, and making each of its parts a subordinate or derivative god, as the sun, the moon, the stars, the earth, the winds, the waters. It then supplemented these gods, to suit man's growing depravation, by going down into the impure organic world, and making gods of its trees and animals, its beasts, birds, reptiles, insects, and fishes. Last of all, it deified the most degraded of all things, men divested of all the noble characteristics of humanity involved in the imitation of the character of the one true God; and who masquerade as selfish, crafty, and cruel political and ecclesiastical despots, under the false but most significant colors of seemingly authorized representatives and vicegerents from a supernatural and

cruel monster, described as disregarding all human rights
in his desire to elevate his assuming representatives and
official servants above the masses of mankind, by
making all other men slaves to serve his pretended favorites. Thus the scale of Oriental idols runs down from
sun gods, moon gods, star gods, beast gods, fish gods,
bird gods, snake gods, to the base man gods of political
and ecclesiastical despotism.

This Oriental error, which still pervades, in its elementary form of monism, much of modern so-called
science and philosophy, results from carelessly ignoring
the primary truth taught by the sensuous ideas, that
spirit differs, in every respect, as an active agent, from
matter as a passive means and instrument, subservient to
the spirit's action; so that the spirit, whether of man or of
God, differs, as active subject, from its immediate object,
which must be matter; as matter is the medium by which
the action of spirit is received and conducted or trans-
mitted by the subject. By neglecting the nature of the
principles of science, as uniformities of God's action, or
laws of God, exhibited in matter, as something moved by
him, and therefore altogether different from him, this
error not only precludes all physical science, which must
cease to be science when its matter is spiritualized,
and is no longer matter; but it also perverts the moral
character of God; who must cease to be a pure spirit or
a good spirit, when he is in any way identified with the
Oriental conception of matter, and is thus materialized.
Hence, this error sets up, instead of the true God, and
widely differing from him, an idol of science, which,

because it is purely imaginary, is incapable of being known.

It is to this revamped error of ancient Orientalism that must be attributed the rise of modern agnosticism, and the establishment of a scientific monotheistic idolatry, with an unknown idol, but with an influence disastrous at once to the progress of science, and to the perfection of all practical social life, which must be the imitation of a known God, of perfect truth and morality.

Notwithstanding, however, the almost universal prevalence of that ancient heathen Oriental error, some of the rules or principles of art, and some principles of the science of mathematics, which in their lower stages are independent of that error, seem to have been early collected, by means of the sensuous ideas, among some ancient nations, especially the Greeks. But it is owing to obstruction from that error that the principles, or laws, of the physical sciences, and the methods of scientific inquiry have only been discovered in modern times, mostly since Francis Bacon. And in all the practical operations of modern society the injurious effects of that error are still being experienced.

Thus, the fundamental error of the republic of letters and art, in the white race, is its failure to clearly and fully apprehend the First Principle of the Kingdom of God; and this error, induced by the ancient error of heathen Orientalism, and injuriously affecting all the interests of society, must necessarily, in a general social reformation, be first corrected.

The white race, although it has partially failed to clearly apprehend the First Principle of the Kingdom of God, has hitherto been mentioned as being the first impersonation of the Kingdom of God; as exemplifying in its practice normal social organization; as the leader of the other races, far in advance of them all, and as distinctively the race of progress. Such, indeed, it is; and as such it holds, in view of its obligation to God, under the social contract, a position of grave responsibility to the other races, both as their natural instructor and as their natural guardian, as their teacher of the truth, and as the protector of their rights.

But it must be remembered that the white race is endowed with liberty; that while liberty is a priceless treasure, its abuse is fraught with unspeakable evils; that this race is as free to lapse into error as it is free to advance toward the truth, as free to do evil as it is free to do right, as free to worship idols as it is free to serve and imitate God; and that without this liberty it would have no approving judgment of truth, and no moral consciousness of merit in its service to God, or in its practical goodness to man.

It should not surprise us, therefore, to find in the white race, as the result of the abuse of its liberty, occasional instances of temporary degradation in error and crime, both individual and national; and instances extending, in the case of nations and even of the whole race, over tracts of centuries and millenniums of debasement. Against the repetition of these lapses, we are morally bound, knowing the cause of such disasters to be a departure from the principles of the Kingdom of God, to provide, by a timely and general social reformation, an adequate remedy.

For individuals, nations, and the race, are always free to resume, by repentance, their place in the Kingdom of God. While error and crime are departures from the First Principle, repentance is a return to it.

The departure from the First Principle by mankind in general led to almost universal error and crime, which culminated, as we have seen, in ancient heathenism, comprised in despotism, idolatry, and sacerdotalism, and maintained by ignoring the social contract. It resulted in offensive wars of conquest and subjugation, with consequent domestic as well as political and ecclesiastical slavery in the masses of the people, throughout the known world. Then was preached in the white race the noted call to repentance, and a new era of hope and of ultimate civilization and liberty was inaugurated by the proclamation of the Kingdom of God.

At that time, the white race commenced a glorious career of progress; but it soon lapsed again into grave heathen errors and crimes, which now again call for repentance and reform. The necessity for immediately heeding this call is manifest.

For, judging from the net result of the alternate progress and retrogression of the white race, even since the beginning of the new era, not to speak of the danger of a prolonged positive relapse, it would require, at the slow rate of the absolute progress of the race, a millennium before the error of Orientalism can be entirely disentangled and eliminated, in the speculative and practical action of modern civilization, from the First Principle. Hence the necessity for directing universal attention to that principle and for working up its universal revival, as the first step of the community, or society, into the Kingdom of God.

This revival must be scientific, philosophic, and even in part metaphysical,—engaging not merely the emotions, but the highest reasoning powers of the learned; while it is taken up and followed out, by means of the sensuous ideas, in the instinctive thought, and in a rational public opinion, of the masses of the people.

When the republic of letters and art has measurably discarded the fundamental Oriental error, which still dwarfs and perverts its energy, it will be free, as the predominantly speculative, and the leading integral organ of society, to develop from the First Principle, and to teach in its universities and other institutions of learning, for the benefit of all the predominantly practical integral organs of society, not only all derivative, speculative and practical principles, but the whole implied scheme of the social contract.

While the discovery, elaboration, and teaching of all principles belong properly to the republic of letters and art, the practical application of these principles is the appropriate work of the other integral organs. Leaving, therefore, the republic of letters and art, for its part of the proposed general social reform, to develop and to free from heathen Oriental influence the First Principle, we will glance at the leading practical errors in the other integral organs that need a remedy.

77. In the republic of the church, the religious integral organ of society, the most prominent practical error prevailing in by far the greater portion of it, apart from its mere dogmatic errors, resulting from the false

Oriental heathen teaching of the republic of letters and art, is its abnormal organization. This is the self-constituted, non-representative ring, adopted from the forms of heathen despotism, and opposed to the normal general form of social organization, called civil representative democracy.

The supposed basis of this fundamental practical error of the republic, or integral organ, of the church, is the assumption that its permanent so-called heavenly type, the Kingdom of God in heaven, is analogous to a human despotic government; and that God is consequently to be regarded as an absolute monarch, or despot, issuing arbitrary commands for man to obey.

But the laws of God are not His commands; otherwise, men could not fail always to obey them. His laws are the uniformities of His action; and it is by His action towards men, that God shows them what they should do to each other. It is not by words, an imperfect invention of man, but by perfect acts, that God tells men what they should do. There is in man's nature an innate nobility, as well as a tendency to imitation, that leads him, when he sees a perfect ideal or example of conduct, to do what is right. When man knows God, he can not fail voluntarily to attempt, to the extent of his ability, to imitate Him. Being free, it would not be right to drive him by irresistible commands, which would take his freedom away. The moral restraints upon man's actions are their rational and easily foreseen immediate consequences, in which consists the discipline of God. Besides, if God, for any purpose, had ever literally spoken to man, or addressed him otherwise than by His Providential actions, He would do so now, for God is unchangeable.

The explanation of the fact, that in very ancient times the laws of God, as the Ten Commandments, and the two Great Commandments, were put into the form of commands, is that, in those times, heathen, Oriental despotic government being almost everywhere established, and most human laws being issued in the form of despotic commands, God, who was represented as a despot, was also supposed in His law-giving to imitate the usual earthly despotic forms. Hence, those persons who were then believed to have learned, in any way, the will of God, and who consequently felt justified in saying before the people, "Thus saith the Lord," were led to put their honest conception of His will into what was generally received as the most forcible, and the most appropriate, official form, which evidently must then have been the form of a despotic command.

All normal human society has been shown to be the association of God with man, based on an original and continuing social contract between God and man. The conception, first, of the Kingdom of God, and then of the church, in imitation of it, as a rule or government of God over man, is a purely heathen, Oriental, despotic, and sacerdotal invention. It is the contrivance of some ancient, forgotten ring of office-seekers and place-hunters; but surviving, like other rings, in the consequences of its evil deeds. It is a scheme designed to create a number of well-paid priestly, or sacerdotal, public offices, parallel in their emoluments, and in public estimation and influence, with the class of political offices; thus throwing a double burden on the people.

Although, at first, the political offices of the ancient despotism, including the office of the despot himself, were primarily supported by military power, and the sacerdotal offices by idolatry and superstition, both supports afterwards became blended, and both classes of public officers afforded to each other mutual protection; until, in Christendom, in the middle ages, the sacerdotal officers attempted, by usurped political power, to subordinate to themselves the political officers, or the political government.

It was in times of general ignorance that the sacerdotal or ecclesiastical officers, calling themselves the church, overcame by their so-called spiritual, or rather superstitious weapons, the temporal weapons of the political government of the state; and asserted for themselves, in the name of the church, but without any authority from the people, a paramount government, with despotic temporal power, over the whole world. Since the thirteenth century, however, in proportion to the increase of public intelligence in Christendom, the governmental authority, the so-called temporal power, of the ecclesiastical officers of the church, the hierarchy, has gradually declined.

But, until very recently, in the second half of the present century, the head, or Pope of the hierarchy, or body of ecclesiastical officers of the larger portion of the Christian church, the Roman Catholic, has maintained, with few interruptions, at Rome, over a circumscribed mass of Italian political subjects, a despotic throne, shorn, indeed, of the splendor of much of the temporal power it formerly symbolized beyond the limits of Italy, but distinctly foreshadowing the hope of that hierarchy to resume and extend over the whole world the full measure of its former temporal power.

If the Pope has temporal power, as he claims, he is clearly a despot; for there is no constitution emanating from the people to limit his power, nor is he elected by the people, or by representatives of the people. If the temporal power claimed by the Pope and the hierarchy is lawful, the Italians and the rest of the world are not entitled to liberty. But if the Italians and the rest of the world are entitled to liberty, as one of the boons of Christianity, the temporal power claimed by the Pope and the hierarchy is not lawful.

The hierarchy, in claiming temporal power, is not only plainly aiming to set up a temporal government of the hierarchy in opposition to the spiritual Kingdom of God, but is also engaged, in opposition to the temporal rights and liberty of the people, in a direct conflict against the principle of civil representative democracy.

Both Saint Peter and Saint Paul, far from being mere ecclesiastical shams and make-believes, are proved by unquestionable records to have been honorable gentlemen, as well as saints, in the best sense of those words; and doubtless, in imitation of the master, whom they openly and honestly professed to follow, they would have scorned to claim a temporal power involving necessarily a government "of this world," which he disclaimed. Nor is it possible to prove, that any unsophisticated follower of Saint Peter or Saint Paul, or of their common master, can consistently claim, in his ecclesiastical capacity, any temporal power in opposition to the political government of the state.

An ecclesiastical ring, with its government, is not peculiar to one religious denomination. It is found alike among Jews, Mohammedans and Christians, Roman Catholics and Protestants; except some Christian denominations which have advanced to clearer notions of the proper separation and independence of the church from the state and of the state from the church. Wherever there is an order of clergy separate from, and claiming superiority to, the laity, there are the rudiments of an ecclesiastical ring with its government, which, although it may at present be impotent in deed, is evil in its tendency.

If the Christian church, in all its divisions, or branches, will reject its ecclesiastical ring and ecclesiastical government, and adopt a normal organization of the church, according to the general organizing principle of civil representative democracy; electing by the people of each of its denominations, respectively, those whom each chooses to honor and support as its religious leaders, teachers, and officers; the whole church, by fair representation, can easily be united in one organization, under the general Christian tradition, as one Christendom, combining all the religious zeal, the calm piety, and the saintly devotion of the whole Christian body, as an example to be followed by the other sections of the universal church.

The discussion leading to this result ought not to be made to hinge on names of ecclesiastical distinctions that have been heretofore acrimoniously used. But even the old sectarian shibboleths that are employed to express and hedge different shades of religious belief or diversities of religious ceremonial and office—as Roman Catholic, Old Catholic, Greek, Protestant, Presbyterian, Baptist, Methodist, bishop, archbishop, presbyter, priest, pope, deacon, elder, minister, pastor—may be emptied of their uncharitable implications, and made to do good service in designating indifferent outward forms of highly important things that are, respectively, essentially the same at heart.

Even the word priest, which to many persons smacks strongly of heathenism and of the old dispensation, because it is used to translate the classical and the Hebrew words that signify the bloody, butchering sacrificers of innocent animals, and even of men, upon the ancient altars, is a perfectly innocent Anglo-Saxon contraction of the familiar New Testament word presbyter, which simply means elder.

When, by separating entirely, in a normal organization of society, the integral organ of the church from the integral organ of government, and assigning to each what properly belongs to it and no more, the mock ecclesiastical governments and their feuds are dispensed with, there will be a reign of religious toleration and peace. The social communion under one organization of the different religious denominations will not be prevented by their various false dogmas, which will then be left to the enlightened discussion and calm judgment of the republic of letters and art, to be finally settled in conformity with the First Principle.

At the same time, the numerous benevolent and charitable orders and associations supported by those denominations can be united with others in their common charitable and benevolent aims in the integral organ of charity.

78. The next practical error to be considered is an error of organization in the republic, or integral organ, of industry, leading to the prevailing general industrial anarchy, or industrial war. The practical error of the republic of industry is two-fold. First, it neglects the separation of its general organization from the other integral organs, and especially from the integral organ of government; which, from ancient heathen times to the present, has uniformly degraded, to the ultimate injury of all the industrial classes, the class of working-men; who, under the ancient despotic governments, were slaves, under the feudal governments were serfs, and under the modern governments are impoverished by monopolies, privileges, and so-called protection, granted to a few favorites. Secondly, it fails to secure among all the industrial classes a co-operative union and organization based on the identity, in the long run, of their respective interests.

The integral organ, or republic of industry, consists of four distinct industrial classes, ideally separate and integrally connected; each, therefore, interpenetrating the rest, and all interoperating with each other—the working-men, the employers, the capitalists, and the consumers. In a higher state of society than the present, the interests of the working-men and employers will be considered so absolutely identical as to constitute them one class, that of labor, the employers representing the highest grade of skilled labor; as in a still higher state of society the interests of all the industrial classes will be regarded as identical. But for the present the four industrial classes named above will be treated as distinct from each other.

In the arrangement of these classes, sex is here unnoticed. Working men include working women; as entitled to the same rights; and if it be said by the men that most women are not producers, and are not concerned in the general interests of productive industry, but are properly limited to domestic work, the reply is, that the domestic women as a class are the mothers of the producers, and for this reason should be eminently respected, and comfortably supported, in their domestic work, by the men.

Seemingly, the evil effects of the two-fold practical error of the republic of industry are felt exclusively by the class of working-men, whose loud complaints of wrongs are heard, and whose multitudinous unions and associations for obtaining redress are seen, throughout the civilized world. But, as separate and distinct classes, the employers, capitalists, and consumers suffer also, in many instances, and in many respects, from the same error. For the result of that two-fold error is the prevailing universal industrial war, which threatens with disaster and unsettles every industrial interest. In this war, as in other wars, a few individuals, who in this war are capitalists and employers, may heap up plunder; but among the multitudes disabled and stripped upon the industrial battle-field are many who have been

generous employers and liberal capitalists, and are compelled to surrender to the temporary victors of their
own class the honest accumulations of a well-spent life,
and the very business by which they trusted to gain a
livelihood.

Yet, passing by the grievances of capitalists and employers, let us see what remedy can be applied to right
the wrongs of the working-men. For, if it does justice
to these, it must equally benefit the other classes. The
industrial elements, which all live alongside of each other
in society, like adjoining tribes, are labor, the business
capacity of employers, capital and consumption. Each
of these elements is indispensable to the rest. The
present industrial policy, which has led to the present
industrial war, is to arm each of these elements by a
hostile threatening combination against all the others.
This is the policy of ancient, heathen, offensive, conquering war; by which one tribe, instead of cultivating
with each adjoining tribe neighborliness and commercial
intercourse, which would enrich both, invades it, con-
quers it, robs it, enslaves it. Industry is a machine,
and the interest of all its parts is to keep it going, for
when one part stops, the whole stops. So, when consumers strike, or boycott the producer, by refusing to
purchase goods, or by insisting on getting them for cost
or less, at a bargain;—that stops production, and injures
labor, capital and employer; when capital strikes, or
gets timid and withdraws from business;—that injures
labor, employer and consumer; when employers strike,
or lock out, or reduce wages;—that injures labor, capital
and consumer; and when labor strikes, that injures labor,

employer, capital and consumer.   Thus, the working-
men suffer by every stoppage of industry, no matter
whose strike is the cause; and every industrial class can
strike, and when it pleases, does strike.   It is evident,
therefore, that the remedy for the evils suffered by the
working-men must be the stoppage of those strikes,
which are the battles of the industrial war; and it is
equally evident that these battles, like the battles in
every other war, can only be stopped by negotiation,
through representatives of the parties to it, resulting in
a treaty or contract among them.

An industrial treaty of peace, then, among all the
industrial classes, adopted deliberately and based on
rational conditions, is the remedy demanded by the interests of them all, and especially of the working-men.
But to accomplish a wise treaty leading to beneficial and
permanent industrial peace, it is not enough for the
contending parties to be banded or brigaded in hostile
armies; they must have a civil and national organization
which can appoint duly authorized agents to conduct
and conclude negotiations for peace.   Mere military
bodies can at most make a temporary truce.

In order to bring about an industrial peace, it is
necessary for the republic of industry to correct its two-
fold practical error, preparatory to disbanding its hostile
and threatening combinations, its armies; and, after
separating itself from the government, to establish for
itself, in the way already pointed out, according to the
principle of civil representative democracy, a normal
social organization of all its industrial classes.   This organization would include a general industrial legislature;

the resolutions of which, as industrial positive law, would bind all the industrial classes, and place them, in regard to each other, in normal and equitable relations.

The preliminary steps to this organization could be taken by some concerted action of organized labor inviting to a conference with its representatives the representatives of the numerous large organized bodies of employers and capitalists; or the invitation to a conference could come from the other side; or, if neither of these hostile parties would make the first move, the consumer, as the equally interested body of the general public, could proceed, of its own motion, to effect the necessary general industrial organization.

It should be particularly noticed in the republic of industry, that, according to the Semitic philosophy, every normal association, by taking the First Principle as its guide, virtually has God as a leading or controlling member, and according to his known will, must seek not only its own, but also the public welfare, in conformity with the general social contract.

It may also be added, that as all legitimate capital, besides the direct gifts of God, originally consists in the labor and wages saved by the working-man, there also belongs to the working-man, according to his skill, industry, and character, the opportunity to become an employer and a capitalist; and that, accordingly, while many if not most of the employers are or have been working-men, a large proportion of the vast capital of the savings banks belongs to working-men, or has been accumulated by them for their families. But, in addition to the opportunities of advancement open to the individual working-man, it is plain that if a large number of work-ing-men known to each other will associate themselves as a corporation, under capable directors of their own choice, and will pool their labor and their savings, as a labor bank, which, if well managed, would soon take the place of the present savings banks, they can advance their savings in suitable sums, well secured, and their labor of different kinds in gangs, by contracts guaranteed on both sides against strikes, and in other respects, on business principles, to employers of labor. Thus, work-ing-men, by bringing their own labor and their own cap-ital into profitable co-operation, can not only place their capital in friendly competition with other capital, but can also influence in their favor, and at the same time greatly benefit, such employers as they approve.

Such labor banks, ably conducted, would be highly conservative. They would practically secure the har-mony, and thereby demonstrate the identity, of the inter-ests of all the industrial classes; furnishing capital to the employers, and work to the working-men, and thus enlarging, for the benefit of other capitalists and of the consumers alike, the scope of the general business of transportation and distribution; while, according to the principles of industrial economy, as distinguished from so-called political economy, the dangers of overproduc-tion would be avoided by the industrial statistics, and the facility of intercommunication and consultation among the producers, which would be furnished by the normal general organization of the republic of industry.

In contrast with the conservative general industrial organization, and its labor banks of working-men, as above described, the radical socialistic notion of vesting all capital in the government should receive a passing notice. A few obvious considerations will show that the socialistic scheme based on this notion opposes the social contract, by pauperizing the masses, and thus depriving individuals of the power to charitably help their fellow-men; as it would cut off the career of advancement of the industrious, intelligent, prudent, and moral working-man, by compelling all to share the same lot with the idle, improvident, and sensual—the evident lot of ultimate equal pauperism, barbarism, and slavery. For this scheme would make the government the sole capitalist, and virtually the sole or chief employer, without any competition to check the rapacity of the central political ring, which necessarily, on account of the extreme complication of the machinery of the government, would rule with despotic power, and would doubtless repeat the old story of the many governed and utilized by the few. Thus, this scheme would intensify, in the highest degree, the very evils now charged to the hostile combination of capital and employers against labor; but which, it has been shown, may be entirely removed by the rational harmonious action of all the industrial classes.

79. The practical error of the integral organ, or republic, of public charity, besides its omission to complete its separate general organization, in the form already indicated, is its failure, in cases of aggravated and widespread moral delinquency, threatening great public disaster, to invoke, in support of its efforts for public

moral reform, the aid of the moral authority, fortified by the physical power, of the government.

In early rude societies, merely moral offences are not generally noticed; public crimes are of few kinds, and the public moral reformer does not walk abroad. New kinds of crimes, because not at first regarded as such, are for a long time committed, not only with impunity, but also without reproach; until public conscience, disclosing their true nature, modifies in regard to them the public opinion, and the public opinion modifies the public law, causing it to declare them criminal, and, as such, punishable. From time to time, in the progress of society, some apparently merely moral delinquencies of little seeming public interest, have from changing circumstances in the environment of society, become dangerous to the social order; and the government has felt itself bound to stigmatize them as public crimes, and to impose upon them severe punishments.

For instance, when personal property was of small comparative value, and was usually kept in the owner's immediate possession, almost the only crimes recognized by the old law, in regard to personal property, were larceny, or private stealing, and robbery; as they involved a fraudulent or forcible taking away of personal property from the possession of the owner, against his will. But, if the owner voluntarily parted with the possession of personal property, there was no public crime committed when the person to whom it was entrusted converted it to his own use. For a breach of trust was not then regarded as a criminal offence, but a mere moral delinquency.

But, when transactions of trade, that required the money or other personal property of one person to be entrusted to another, increased in number and importance, breaches of trust became an injury to the public, and they were considered as violations of the higher law of principle, and as illegal. Positive laws were then enacted by the government to declare them public crimes, and to impose upon them definite punishments. So, there are many other acts that were formerly committed with impunity, and, in the case of duelling, with even decided public approbation, that have now been stigmatized and are punished by the law, as odious public crimes.

From the experience of the past, it must be considered probable, that, with the advance of society in intelligence, in religion, and in morality, and with the increasing complication of human affairs, requiring their regulation by the far reaching and consistent system of the First Principle, other instances of acts committed now, not only with impunity, but without any suspicion of their criminality, by multitudes of individuals, will be found, on examination, to be highly injurious to the public, and as such both immoral and of evil public example, or criminal. Such acts, in an enlightened community, by whomsoever committed, even by individuals in criminal ignorance of the criminality of their acts, must be condemned in the public conscience, not only as private immoral practices, but also as public wrongs in violation of the social contract; because these acts are injurious to the public, while the social contract requires that all acts, whether of individuals or of

associations, must, if not indifferent, conduce to the
public welfare.

But, when the public conscience is thoroughly awak-
ened in regard to acts of individuals producing any
public wrong, it will steadily direct the public opinion
of the people to the practical steps necessary to prevent
such acts. Nor can it be doubted that a moderate law
called for by the public conscience for this purpose,
declaring such acts of individuals to be criminal and
punishable, will be enforced with all the power of the
aroused public conscience, and of the enlightened and
instructed public opinion of the people, so as to prevail triumphantly among their masses; and that the
opposers of it, however self-sufficient in their own private estimation, will be publicly set down among the
other criminal classes, and will be treated accordingly.

That intoxication or drunkenness is a monstrous public evil, and that, being voluntarily or intentionally
inflicted, it is a grave public wrong, is undoubted.
Equally certain is the fact, that it is the use of intoxicating drinks or drugs by individuals, that produces this
public wrong. The conclusion is inevitable that the act
of individuals in using intoxicants, in itself, and as an
evil public example, is criminal. It is a mistaken
notion to regard the makers and sellers of intoxicants as
exclusively responsible for the public evil caused by their
use. The makers and sellers of intoxicants are guilty as
aiders and abettors of the crime of those that use them;
but the principal criminals, primarily guilty of the great
public wrong voluntarily inflicted on the public by intoxication or drunkenness, are those by whom intoxicants

arc used. For, if intoxicants were not used, they would not be made, and they could not be sold, to produce intoxication; although they might be made and sold for an innocent purpose, as for use in the arts.

When the public conscience becomes aware of the true state of the case, and sees who are the most guilty parties in the perpetration of the public wrong of general intoxication, it will stir up the public opinion to frame and enforce a stern but moderate law placing the use of intoxicants among the most baneful public crimes. It may seem to many a harsh measure, to forbid by law what they esteem the agreeable stimulation caused by the use of intoxicating drinks; but, when society has advanced to a higher plane of cultured civilization by stamping out the crime of intoxication, with all its brutalizing consequences, the proposition to allow the use of intoxicants, and thus to debauch the rising pure generation, would shock the community quite as much as would a proposition now to restore the former impunity for breaches of trust, and to place the vast accumulations of capital in public institutions, as well as the funds of private individuals, at the mercy of those entrusted with them; so that they could do with them as they please, without the fear of criminal prosecution for the breach of their trust by embezzlement.

Intoxication having been handed down to us as a relic of ancient Oriental heathenism, being described in the Vedas, the oldest religious books of the Aryan race, as a part of the ceremonial worship of a god of intoxication, called Soma in those books, Dionysos by the Greeks, and Bacchus by the Romans, a strong effort for its abolition is a plain duty of the integral organ, or republic of public charity, the integral organ of Christian society that is charged with the work of moral reform.

But, while the republic of public charity, to aid its practical efforts and moral suasion to this end, is entitled to call upon the government to perform its duty in this respect by the enactment of proper criminal legislation, it is equally entitled to require it to abstain from interference with the proper work of the integral organ of public charity, either by illegal and extravagant perversion of public funds, contributed for governmental purposes, to ill-advised and pernicious almsgiving, as in pensions not fairly earned; or by enforcing with the power of the government the pretensions of one class of citizens demanding, as sturdy beggars, gratuitous contributions from the rest. For neither are alms illegally lavished from an overflowing treasury, nor are contributions from the poor exacted by governmental force for the benefit of the craving rich, charity, and as little are they justice; but they tend not only to pauperize the masses, but also to demoralize the whole of the community.

Intolerance, being the greatest enemy to charity, should be altogether banished from the whole integral organ, or republic of charity. · The different charitable and benevolent associations in each of the five general classes of associations that are assigned, respectively, for relieving the strain and facilitating the normal work of each of the five integral organs of society, should then combine in the general organization of its class, without regard to the religious distinctions prevalent in the separate associations. This action would produce a powerful concentration of charitable force in each of five parallel lines of charitable effort. These lines, by an extension of liberal culture, with increasing human sympathy, according to the general drift of the First Principle, can then be drawn, by the attraction of mutual love, to converge to one center of integral charitable power. This could be made to bear harmoniously, at once, by instruction, moral and religious inspiration, industrial employment, material aid with friendly encouragement, and governmental justice, on the eradication of the roots of immorality and crime, sprung from uncultured monotheistic idolatry, and growing from the soil of ignorance, irreligious, immoral, unsympathetic social conversation, destitution, and the enticing impunity of gross offenders.

The present lack of organization is most important in the class of charitable associations intended to co-operate with the government. One branch of these would aid the ultimate purpose of the government by converting the punishment into the reformation of criminals; while another branch would promote, in practical social intercourse, the general cultivation of the social ideals, by providing first-rate, æsthetic, rational, and cheap public entertainments.

It will then be seen that charity is as paramount as the apostle describes it; and that, by completely organizing it, society will thoroughly humanize and reform itself.

80. In the republic of government the practical error of faulty organization not only prevails in its action as

a whole, by its usurping functions of the other integral organs; but also both by the absence of normal organization and by the prevalence of abnormal organization in each of its four partial organs, and in its extraordinary undenominational governmental representative assembly, or convention. The usurpation by it of functions of other integral organs has been explained. The partial organs of the government, as before mentioned, are (a) its political parties; (b) its ordinary governmental legislature; (c) its body of executive officers, and (d) its legal profession.

81. (a) Political parties are the outward mechanism of the people's collective thought, leading to their collective practical action. They are based on the truism that every question has two sides, while some questions have more than two. Every struggle of political parties involves a public debate, in which each party embraces one side of the leading question of immediate and controlling public interest, and brings into the general discussion all pertinent arguments in support of its side; so that every individual citizen, by giving due attention to the arguments of all the political parties, can determine understandingly the side with which he agrees, and can then give practical effect to his determination by his vote.

As political parties, with the First Principle, have all principles in common, the questions on which political parties differ cannot be questions of principle; but must be applications of principle, or practical measures. For the same reason, political parties as distinguished from factions, must be honorable associations; and as normal

associations, each must have as its end the general welfare of the public.

It must be remembered that the people can act collectively otherwise than as political parties. There are
questions which, in private judgment, can have more
than one side—as questions regarding action towards a
public enemy, or the discharge of public obligations; but
which, in their public aspect, can have but one proper
issue, can lead to but one set of patriotic measures.
There are also elections held for public offices that are
entirely unconnected with the questions debated by
political parties. There are likewise periods when the
proper work of existing political parties, or of those
which have chiefly divided the public, seems, by the final
adoption or rejection of their respective practical measures, to be accomplished; and when, accordingly, the public attention, looking away from those measures, and from
the parties which have supported or contested them, is
variously directed either to questions hitherto regarded
as of secondary importance, but now claiming the first
rank of public interest; or to questions newly emerging
on the horizon of the boundless and ever moving sea of
public debate; so that individuals, without regard to
their former political affiliations, will be grouped around
these new questions, and will form new parties for the
support or rejection, respectively, of the practical measures which these questions suggest. In all these cases
the people will be compelled, for a time, to act independently of the organization of any political party, and
entirely upon their own individual responsibility. Thus

we see the limit to which the proper action of political parties extends, and beyond which it cannot go.

The organization of a political party, like that of every other large association, is designed to produce the intelligent and concerted action of its members. Its intelligent action can only be promoted by the free intercourse and conference of its members. Its concert of action can only be effected by means of fair representation, by reliable delegates, duly authorized to act for it by its primary meetings, and uniting in a central representative meeting for deliberation and joint action.

The prevalent abuses of the organizations of political parties are two-fold. In the first place, no provision is made for the free public intercourse and habitual conference with each other of the members of each party, in their primary neighborhoods, whenever so disposed. Hence, the individuals composing the masses of a party hardly ever meet each other except on the day of an election, and then only to ratify by their votes the action taken in their name by a few persons without actually consulting them. It is probable, that this abuse has arisen from the fact that, in the beginning of a political party, a few persons, by their strenuous advocacy of its measures, and by their untiring activity in executing its behests, acquire, as they deserve, its almost unbounded confidence, and are almost exclusively entrusted with the management of its affairs; and that afterwards, in various ways, other persons succeed to the position and authority of these original managers, without having the same titles to the party's regard. Thus, the masses of the party are led to take final action by their vote, without previously taking together any preparatory counsel. In the next place, this abuse leads to the formation within the party of the other consequential, or rather connate and twin abuse, of a non-representative governing, or despotic, ring. The ring is formed by the most ancient despotic device of governing the many by the few. Consultation on the general affairs of the party being dispensed with, the attendance on the primary meetings is small, and can always be controlled by a few trained retainers in the interest of a smaller few, constituting the ring. Such are the prevalent two-fold abuses of the organization of political parties.

The obvious remedy for both of these abuses is to provide in each neighborhood, or smallest locality in which primary political meetings are held, convenient houses with separate rooms, as permanent places in which, at all seasons, the members of each political party may meet by themselves for consultation and counsel in advance of the regular periods for making nominations of candidates, and for elections; so that the general body of members, the militia, of each party, may have an opportunity both to become acquainted with each other's views, and to be well informed of all significant movements having a political bearing, whether within or without the party; and thus to be quite as well prepared as the trained bands of the ring, not only for sending reliable delegates to the nominating conventions, but also for casting their votes at the general elections.

The arrangement of these neighborhood houses, and of corresponding central houses, the rules for apportioning their apartments to the different political parties, for loaning them, by courtesy, to other associations and to the public for occasional meetings, and the propriety of furnishing them with books and papers, need not detain us.

The importance of encouraging the conference of the members of a political party in its several neighborhoods, by providing the proper means for it, will be apparent, when the magnitude of the public evils caused by the ring, and brought about by the want of those conveniences, is considered.

The First Principle, and the social contract founded upon it, the public conscience, and the private conscience of each individual, all teach that it is the duty of every citizen towards his fellow citizens to act, and therefore to vote, honestly. He is bound to vote with his best and most deliberate judgment, intelligently, if he can; but at all events honestly. Montesquieu, in his book entitled "Spirit of the Laws," published a little before the middle of the eighteenth century, asserts that the peculiar and distinguishing principle of a republic is virtue.

This position has been abundantly proved by others. But the ring of a political party directly antagonizes the fundamental principle of the republic, by habitually engaging, and using for the accomplishment of its criminal ends, mercenary, that is dishonest, votes; thus corrupting the political life of the people, and thereby committing the highest political crime. For this action of the ring attacks and impairs the sovereignty of the people, a crime for which the people, in self-defense, are justified in inflicting the highest punishment. The legal action of the people is declared by the honest votes cast at an election; the ring undertakes to nullify and defeat the action of the people by dishonest votes. The ring thus engages in a conflict with the people, and it should be prepared, when clearly convicted, to suffer the penalty of its high crime.

The bribes used by the ring to corrupt voters are of several different kinds. They are public offices, public contracts or jobs, and public legislation for private benefit, besides money directly paid as bribes to voters.

The public offices in which the ring deals are of two classes. The first class are the leading elective political offices, by which the general policy and administration of the government are shaped. In disposing of these offices the worst and most insidiously demoralizing influence of the ring is developed. These offices form the legitimate career of all seeking political distinction among their fellow citizens, and the privilege of doing service to the public. They should be open to the fair competition of every honorable ambition, and especially to the generous aspirations of the young, who may be encouraged in their political aims by the sympathy, the approbation, and the public spirit of their neighbors. But the candidates for these offices are soon made aware, that unless they are willing to do disgraceful homage to the ring, by pledging their official action to serve its ends, they will meet its irresistible opposition. Hence, the ring, except in the case of strong personalities and great talents that have acquired a wide popularity independent of its influence, can use the promise of those offices to bribe aspirants.

The other class of public offices used as bribes by the ring are those which have no connection with the avowed policy of any political party—this policy being usually based on national political questions—and which offices can be equally well administered for the interest of the public by any incumbent, otherwise properly qualified, without regard to his political opinions. Such are judicial offices, clerkships of the courts, sheriffalties, mayoralties of cities, and other leading municipal offices, besides the great array of purely ministerial executive offices that are disposed of by the ring as the spoils of party victory, in pursuance of its bargain with the class of leading elective political officers. Such of these non-political offices as are elective are disposed of by the ring in the same way as the class of elective political offices properly connected with political parties, and with the same exceptions, by prostituting and utilizing the organization of political parties in elections that should be independent of it. The remaining offices of this class, being the purely ministerial executive offices that are conferred by the appointment of elective executive chiefs, are distributed according to the influence, and the antecedent bargains, of the ring with those chiefs, express or implied, concerning them.

The resources of the ring for bribery by public contracts or jobs, have been much curtailed by the open public competition for them demanded by public opinion. But public legislation for private benefit continues to be an unmitigated source of public grievance and of widespread corruption.

The money directly paid by the ring to bribe voters, and contributed in large sums by persons of great wealth, who also claim to be highly respectable, but who, if they have even a small measure of intelligence, must know that it will be expended for that purpose, is a foul insult to the majesty, as well as a bold attack upon the sovereignty, of the people. It may be, and it seems probable, that rings in both of the great political parties are guilty of this crime. If so, the honest members of both political parties should unite to bring the guilty to condign punishment. For, it must be repeated, that political parties, as distinguished from factions, are honorable associations.

To check these briberies on the part of the ring, and to preserve equality among the members of political parties, the expenses of each party should be kept within narrow limits, and confined to strictly legitimate and necessary objects; should be defrayed by nearly equal and small contributions, or assessments upon every member able to pay them, and should be exactly recorded in a regular system of accounts; nor should any member be allowed to impose obligations on his fellow members by larger contributions; nor should any candidate be expected to pay more than any other member of the party towards the expenses of an election held to promote the views and interests of the party.

When the ring performs its work, its leaders are rarely seen. Its common members are indistinguishable from the crowd. For all that are not within it, the ring is

invisible, impersonal, a mere chimera of the imagination, a thing "without a local habitation or a name."
Yet, in reality, it is an ubiquitous, despotic institution,
exerting upon political parties vast, oppressive, degrading and malignant power.

The ring, as it uses dishonorable means, does not
belong to the party, but is a potent unseen faction within
it,—a baleful parasitic growth. It preys upon the vitals
of the party; and it compels those portions of it which it
cannot corrupt to become, however reluctantly, its tools,
by voting for its nominees, on what is called the party's
ticket.

The registration, however exact, of voters, and the
secret deposit, however guarded, of votes, are no protection
against either the legion of bribed actually registered
voters, or the unlimited number of unregistered votes, at
the command of the ring, while it controls the machinery
of the party's organization.   There can be no purity of
election, no party action at once honorable and efficient,
until the ring, the despotic, non-representative scheme to
rule by force or fraud the many by the few, is extinguished.
Nor can this be done except by abolishing dishonesty,
with the present facilities for dishonesty, in politics.

It is idle to inveigh against the ring.   It thrives upon
maledictions.   Its evil fame invites, by the hope of its
wicked aid, the strong support of the unscrupulous hosts
that seek by ignoble means the ends, either of sordid
avarice, or of soaring, as well as of groveling, ambition.

The ring works in darkness, by preparing secretly, in
advance of the primary meetings, their attendance and
their action.   Its secrecy is its strength.   The only way

to destroy the ring, therefore, is to throw the glare of day upon its operations. This can be done by permanently locating the primary meetings in the smallest local neighborhoods, and providing, in the way before described, architectural conveniences for the habitual public intercourse of the honest masses of the party in the intervals between the formal primary meetings which transact the local business of the party. Thus, when these meetings take place, every man knowing his neighbor and his neighbor's views, and no opportunity being presented for secret machinations, the masses of the party, acting with full knowledge of what the occasion demands, can easily overcome, by a fair majority vote, in these probably full, zealous and instructed meetings, the drilled few of the ring.

Although political parties now are chiefly national, they may become, for different objects, Interrace, international, state or provincial, and municipal.

82. (b) The governmental legislature is virtually a union of committees elected, respectively, by the different political parties, and authorized to meet together for joint action; and by such action to bind, as public agents, or representatives, the whole people. The action of the legislature expressing the common resolutions of the people, and resulting from the conference of their authorized agents, is in form as well as in substance a public contract, and, like all contracts, requires for its validity perfect good faith.

Hence, the remarks made before concerning the abnormal action of political parties, and the elimination from them of the pernicious influence of the ring, apply to the legislature.

Governmental legislatures have different local spheres. While in theory they may be Interrace and international, they are, in fact, national, state or provincial, and municipal, the latter embracing rural as well as urban districts.

The defects in the organization of the system of governmental legislatures are conspicuous in the absence of such legislatures for local spheres that greatly need them. The connected system of graduated local legislatures may be called the system of home rule.

The principle of home rule is, that the inhabitants, or citizens, of every local sphere, from a neighborhood to a nation or a race, are competent to determine by legislation all questions relating exclusively to their sphere. Under this principle, there can be no conflict of proper or normal legislation.

France and the British Empire are examples of the violation of this rule. Both have too much central legislation for local affairs. France needs local legislatures for its departments, or provinces, and for its communes. The British Empire requires local legislatures, or parliaments, for England as well as for Ireland, Scotland, and Wales, and for some of its municipal districts, both urban and rural, and especially for the large municipal district of London, which is most unjustly and unaccountably, in view of its vast intrinsic power, deprived of home rule in its exclusively local affairs.

In the United States of America, home rule in practice is generally carried out. But some of the state courts have absurdly ignored the principle of home rule, by deciding that the municipal governments of large cities, as Baltimore and New York, are mere creatures of their state legislatures; whereas, according to that principle of law, the people of any municipal district have a perfect right to set up a municipal government for their exclusively local affairs, quite independent of the state government; while the people of the municipal district are subject to the state government in matters exclusively affecting the state. Hence, municipal constitutions, as distinguished from municipal charters, should be of co-ordinate authority with state constitutions, each in its respective sphere. Likewise Interrace and international legislatures are needed to settle Interrace and international questions.

Another defect in the organization of many governmental legislatures is the inequality of the numbers of the voters represented by the individual members of the legislature.

Of this inequality of representation the most remarkable example is the Senate of the United States. The provision of the Constitution of the United States, which, in violation of the principle of representation, assigns two and only two representatives to each state, is a monumental survival, as slavery was, of ancient abuses which the framers of the Constitution were unable to overcome. It is a part of the ancient despotic system of governing the many by the few. It has made the Senate a blot on the political system of America, and should have been abolished with slavery, its twin political monstrosity.

The provision in the Constitution of the United States forbidding its amendment in the matter of the representation of the small as well as the large states by two members in the Senate, regardless of the difference in the population of the states, is, like slavery, a violation of legal and political principle, or of the higher law. It is a violation of the principle of representation, which demands approximate equality, so far as practicable, in the numbers represented by each delegate. As slavery was a violation of the principle of personal liberty, this provision of the Constitution is a violation of the principle of representation involved in the principle of civil representative democracy, by which alone personal liberty can be effectually protected by the organic and concerted action of the people.

This provision of the Constitution, therefore, is illegal; and justice, as well as a proper sense of self-respect in all the states—for the exercise of illegal authority is more degrading in a moral point of view to him who exercises it than to him who is subjected to it—demands its elimination by a proper amendment. Although it is a mere nullity, as illegal, public convenience requires that in the removal of it the forms of a regular constitutional amendment should be observed.

Approximate equality of representation is all that can be reasonably required, and this can be easily attained. All unnecessary departures from it are violations of principle, and, like all violations of principle, they imply their own condemnation. They prevail so glaringly in some local legislatures in the United States, that they need no further remark, except to say that they are notoriously continued for the benefit of rings of the political parties.

The abuse of governmental legislatures in legislating for the special advantage of individuals, as distinguished from the general public, has already been mentioned in connection with the rings of political parties; but it is also the result of a defect of the general governmental organization. For, if the government keeps strictly within its proper organization, it will not interfere with industrial affairs, which belong exclusively to the integral organ of industry, by which they should be regulated.

But, as it cannot be denied that the government has the right to raise revenue necessary for its proper purposes by duties on imports, it should neutralize the incidental interference with industrial pursuits, caused by such duties, by adjusting them on a sliding scale; imposing the highest duties on articles produced abroad by the lowest rate of wages, and the lowest duties on articles produced abroad by the highest wages. Otherwise, the government, by the incidental protection of such duties to particular industries, not to speak of direct protection to them, would reverse the part played by the sentimental and benevolent highwayman of romance, who remorselessly robbed the rich, but liberally bestowed his gains upon the poor; it would plunder the poor, who are the masses of the people, to enrich the wealthy.

83. (c) The body of executive officers, in the civil service of the people, gives rise to great abuses on account of its defective organization. These abuses have been sufficiently indicated in what has been said concerning the rings in the political parties. They could be avoided by

making the appointments to office dependent on examinations similar to those in the military service, with the same tenure of office, and privilege of promotion.

In the military service, the abuses are those incident generally to standing armies, and in a less degree to standing navies; and they can only be cured by abolishing the standing army and navy, and by substituting for them a properly organized and trained militia, for land and sea service. The European governments would require a preliminary international, or even Interrace agreement for a general disarmament, before they could disband their regular armies and navies. The United States of America would experience the same necessity, in regard to its navy; but no such difficulty need prevent them from substituting at once, for its regular army, the militia, mustering in small quotas from all the states and territories, for short terms of service, aggregating about the same number as the present regular army, to do the same duties, with the same organization, drill, and pay. Under proper regulations, the best material would volunteer; and if only the best were accepted, the service would be a source of honor.

Indeed, the illegal employment of the regular army in executing the Reconstruction Act of Congress, is a sufficient warning that the change cannot be made too soon in the United States.

84. (d) The legal profession also is prevented from doing effectually the duty it owes to the public by a defective organization.

It is evident that the legal profession, or the professional lawyers, those who give legal advice, prepare legal papers, argue and decide cases in court, should, on account of their common interest, as respects both each other and the public, be organized as a national and international, and in time, an Interrace guild.

The legal guild would not be a close corporation, but its membership would be accorded with the utmost liberality to all qualified members of the public, and would include all the legal profession in a normal association.

A notable defect of the partial organization of the legal profession of the United States of America, is that it is chiefly composed of bar associations of several cities, united as a national bar association; but that it is far from including all classes of the legal profession, or all the members of even one class.

Similar defects occur in the partial organizations of the legal profession elsewhere. But all classes of the legal profession,—barristers, counselors, pleaders, conveyancers, attorneys, solicitors, proctors, as well as judges—should be brought under one organization in each nation; so that these national organizations in each race may unite in an international organization, and the international organizations, in time, may combine to form an Interrace organization, whenever this shall be needed.

In this way, the good, bad, and indifferent members of the legal profession will be brought under the uniform regulation and discipline of the majority, composed of its reputable members, for the equal benefit of the profession and of the public. The legal profession would thus become a public guild and a normal association, seeking, besides the benefit of its members, the public welfare.

The association of all the members of the legal profession in one organization, will afford opportunity for general public discussions, among them, of the great legal questions, as they successively arise, that must affect the decision of proposed public measures; and the general agreement of the legal profession on such questions would be a useful guide to the people.

When the legal profession, in its judicial, or official, and in its lay, or practicing branch, shall be systematically organized, its title to be considered as one of the partial organs of government, co-ordinate with the others, will be evident; and its legitimate influence on the conduct of public affairs will be clearly apparent, and fully acknowledged. For like each of the other partial organs of the government, the legal profession, in a particular way, represents the people.

The political parties are, and so represent, the people, bodily; the ordinary governmental legislature is directly or indirectly elected by the people, and so represents them; the body of executive officers represents the people, because in part elected by the people directly, and in part appointed indirectly by the people, as by those directly elected and authorized by the people to do so; while the legal profession, as a committee volunteering to act for the rest of the people, in answering, discussing and deciding questions of law, according to principle, and in preparing legal papers, is tacitly confirmed by them, and in this way represents the people. Indeed, the legal profession is the people, so far as they choose to enter that profession, which is free to them, when they acquire the necessary qualifications;

and the whole people are, to a certain extent, lawyers, inasmuch as they are continually considering and determining, not professionally, but for themselves, the questions of law that are involved in most of the practical measures of every-day life; while only in a few cases they apply for assistance to lawyers by profession. Besides, the official or judicial branch of the legal profession, for whom the lay branch are chiefly aids or assistants, are either directly elected by the people, or are indirectly appointed by them through elective executive officers.

The legal profession, when fitly organized, should and could take care, by proper regulations, to raise the standard of qualification of its members, by insisting on a preparation for them of liberal culture, leading to a supreme regard for principle. For it would require a preliminary study of the science of jurisprudence, the basis of which, as of every science, is the First Principle of the Semitic Philosophy. In its legal aspect, indeed, this First Principle, being, in fact, the basis of the original and continuing social contract, and hence of the general organization of society, of the resulting general organization of society's integral organ of government, and of the separate general organization of the government's partial organ, the legal profession, is most appropriately considered as the scientific foundation of jurisprudence. This First Principle of the Semitic Philosophy, and not the heathen Greek and Roman Stoic natural law, is the Christian natural law, sometimes called the higher law, the universal common law, the perfection of reason, or the law of God; being distinguished, as divine and perfect sovereign equity, from human and imperfect positive law.

Case law should be studied to pursue the development of legal principles realized in practice. The reports are mines in which principles, few and far between, are found, embedded in much poor ore and mere rubbish.

When a principle, or rule, is evolved out of one or more cases, it must be established on grounds of reason, and then the principle, or rule, lives on independently of the cases; and the cases, except the few having a historical interest, may be consigned to oblivion.

A rule, ignorantly adopted, not bottomed on reason, may, according to the debatable maxim "*stare decisis*," be called law, as the implied ground of contracts or other business presumably based on it; but when it is shown to be opposed to principle or reason, it must be disregarded, as conflicting with the higher law.

Positive law, although in ancient heathen despotisms and in their modern imitations it appears in the form of a command, is in normal society that approximates to the scheme of civil representative democracy, a voluntary rule adopted by the people for their social co-operation; and thus it partakes of the nature of a contract. According to the end of the co-operation it is designed to promote, it will differ in each of the integral organs of society. Thus, there is an educational positive law, a religious positive law, an industrial positive law, a charitable positive law, and a governmental positive law. Positive law also has different degrees of generality; as municipal, national, international and Interrace.

The positive law with which the legal profession is primarily concerned, is the governmental. But the skill it acquires in framing and interpreting governmental positive law, may be called into requisition in regard to the positive law of the other integral organs of society. The fact also that the legal profession is required to be versed in the discovery, maintenance, and application of principles, in connection with positive law, causes its members of reputation to be called upon for their opinion and advocacy in all social questions involving principle, not only in all the other partial organs of the government, but also in all the other integral organs of society.

Thus, by the suitable organization of the legal profession, its influence and its usefulness, by its advocacy of principle, will be increased to so great an extent, that a leading part will be assigned to it in that general development of the First Principle which must bring about the next impending great social revolution. Nor would the peculiar work of the legal profession, the introduction of uniformity, system, and brevity in the general written positive law, and the extension of the field of scientific jurisprudence, to embrace the races of mankind, as the units of universal society, with rational Interrace rights and duties, be the least of the benefits which that reformation would produce.

85. Having concluded our examination of the defective organization of the four partial organs of the government, that constitute its denominational organization, we will proceed to the consideration of its defective undenominational organization, or its extraordinary undenominational governmental convention; which, in respect

to the special objects of its call, and according to its general or local sphere, is authorized to exert the reserved sovereign power of the people.

The undenominational organization, or convention, of the government is general or local. Its usual general form needs little change. Its varying local form is so defective that it must be regarded as merely inchoate, and as needing great improvement.

(1) It should be observed that its general form is seldom called into action. But these occasions are commonly preceded by so much general discussion, showing the necessity for a general convention, and designating the points which it will be called on to determine, that the people, without distinction of political parties, can readily assemble in primary meetings, in the usual places, and elect delegates to nominate members of the convention, who will then be elected in the usual way by the votes of the people. It seems, therefore, superfluous here to suggest organic changes in the usual methods of conducting popular elections, since these methods will be as sufficient for the formation of an undenominational convention as for other purposes.

A convention is called undenominational, when all the voters, at the same time, and irrespective of the government's partial organs, which are denominational, vote for or against its call and proposed action. But while the political parties are denominational, and cannot properly divide their vote for or against a convention and its action according to their party lines, there may be pronounced differences of opinion in regard both to the necessity of a convention, and to its proper action; and the respective adherents of these different views may organize themselves in the usual way, for voting in concert both as to the call of a convention, and as to the members to be sent to it. State and national conventions are general; and so would be an international convention, as for the nations of Europe.

(2) The local form of undenominational governmental organization should correspond, in a civil representative democracy, with the government's denominational organization, at least in its elective feature, except that the primary meetings should be undenominational.

The convention exercising the local sovereignty of the people, should be elected by the people, for that purpose, in the locality concerned.

But, in the United States of America, where local undenominational proceedings are of frequent occurrence, regular forms are seldom met with, the bodies of men that assume to act with the authority of local undenominational governmental conventions, exercising the local sovereignty of the people, the so-called lynching companies, or vigilance committees, are mostly tumultuary self-constituted crowds, collected from a comparatively small neighborhood, and banded under a single leader; acting from righteous indignation caused by some gross outrage, and designing to execute upon the offender the swift justice which they believe the regular authorities of the government will either fail to apply, or unreasonably delay.

The reform demanded for the undenominational conventions of local districts of the government, is, that they should be openly elected, upon due notice, from a district composed of several primary neighborhoods, and should proceed deliberately and publicly to exercise the reserved sovereign rights of the people for the district represented by the convention in the mode expressed or implied in its call. Such action then would be revolutionary, but legal. But it should carefully avoid the desultory and undignified disorder of a mob.

CHAPTER VI.

CONCLUSION.

THE special difficulties in the way of realizing the general social reformation, with their remedies; the remedies being summed up in the general pursuit of the First Principle of the Semitic Philosophy.

86. The logical effect of a revival of the Semitic philosophy, as the doctrine of the Kingdom of God, would evidently be a development of the knowledge of its First Principle, with a resulting general spread of liberal culture, and a consequent universal and radical social reformation, exhibited in each of the integral organs of society.

In the integral organ, or republic, of letters and art, there would be an improved system of public education, intellectual, religious, moral, artistic, and industrial, beginning by means of the sensuous ideas, with early childhood, and extending to the finished discipline of the universities. In the republic of the church there would be a normal general representative democratic religious association for divine service, including with liberality and toleration all monotheistic purely religious denominations, and excluding all Christian, Jewish, and Mohammedan ecclesiastical governments. In the republic of industry there would be a normal general industrial organization, with representatives from each of the four industrial classes, of capitalists, employers, working-men, and consumers; the now lacking organization of the consumers being the slumbering industrial force, deeply interested, and fully able, when aroused, to shake off from the community the shackles of the trusts and of all the other abnormal industrial associations. In the republic of charity there would be a general co-operating organization of all classes of charitable and benevolent associations, without distinction as to their religious denominations. Finally, in the republic of government, there would be a harmonious development of its four partial organs—its political parties, its legislature, its body of executive officers, and its legal profession; the latter effectively organized, with its official or judicial branch and its lay or practicing branch, and with a universal and uniform system of law inaugurated and applied by it; both of positive law and of principle, Interrace, as well as international, national and municipal.

It seems that a fitting conclusion of the present discussion, therefore, would be to point out the principal difficulties that now obstruct the attainment of a universal social reformation, and to suggest the proper means for their removal.

87. Of such difficulties there are three, the strong tendency of which to check the normal progress of society clearly marks them, in this connection, for special notice. They are, (1) the general and almost universal prevalence of an unsuspected mode of monotheistic idolatry in all the monotheistic nations; (2) the abuse made of the vast mass of printed books and journals, to

restrict original, free and energetic, instinctive thought; and (3) the undue respect paid to ancestors and predecessors, leading men to tolerate, cherish, and imitate, rather than to correct, the faults of those who went before them. These difficulties and their appropriate remedies will be briefly considered. To the first in order of these difficulties, if not also the first in importance, we now proceed—the prevailing monotheistic idolatry.

88. (1) In the creeds and dogmas of the largest denominations in all the monotheistic churches, Christian, Jewish, and Mohammedan, describing the action of God towards sinful transgressors, there is an unmistakable element of unjust, despotic cruelty, which, if true, would mark the character of God as immoral; but which, as false, creates in imagination, in the place of the true God, a monotheistic false idol.

The tendency of idol worship to promote crime, by giving the sanction of its idol to the immorality it represents, is evident. The brutalizing tendency, therefore, of the prevailing monotheistic idolatry cannot be doubted; and to it can be traced the cruel practice of offensive war and conquest, involving all the highest crimes. · Drunkenness, also, is a moral degradation derived from a similar idolatrous source; it having been originally a part of idolatrous worship. It widely prevails in Christianity, and to a less extent, perhaps, in Judaism; while, to the disgrace of both, in the otherwise inferior system of Mohammedanism, it is so far from being licensed, that it is practically suppressed, by suppressing, not the sale, but the use, of intoxicating drinks.

The remedy for monotheistic idolatry, and all other idolatry, whether Christian, Jewish, or Mohammedan, is to teach God's true character as free from passion, and with its parts or attributes co-operating with each other to form one consistent integral whole of justice and love, or mercy, according to the original Christian conception of his universal Fatherhood. This teaching must exclude all idolatry.

Man's life surely tends to accord with the object of his worship. If that object, however called, is in fact an immoral monotheistic idol, his life will be immoral; and it will be more easily accounted for by his idol, than by an imagined original sin of his first progenitor. But if the object of his worship is the one personal, perfect God, his life will be cultured by his knowledge of God, with or without the learning of books, and it will be virtuous. For worship as required by reason in general, and by religion in particular, is first the knowledge, and then the imitation, of the one personal, perfect God. The responsibility, therefore, of the largest monotheistic religious denominations, from their teaching of the cruel and hence immoral character of God, for the crime prevalent in monotheistic nations, is manifest.

89. (2) The next difficulty in the way of a general social reformation, by means of the First Principle of the Semitic philosophy, as the doctrine of the Kingdom of God, is the abuse, or misuse, of the present stock and the current accumulations of the productions of the press. The abuse of the enormous and increasing store of books and journals, is the failure to systematically criticise and use them.

To describe the universe, or any considerable part of it, fully in writing, would make a mass of books almost as large as the universe or the part described. To write down all the thoughts that pass through men's minds, even for a year, would form a bulk of written matter almost equally large. The books and journals thus written would be worse than useless, although they would contain all science, all philosophy, all poetry, all literature. They would leave no place in the universe for man and his work.

Selection of the contents, and limitation of the production of books and journals, are evidently necessary. Equally necessary are selection and limitation in the use of books and journals actually produced. For few of them are altogether good and useful; while some of them are absolutely worthless, and many are positively bad. Some betray ignorance; others show intentional misrepresentation; some present vice under a veil; others display it in all its nakedness; some disseminate error; others elaborate crime.

In the schools of all kinds, the books should not only be select, but they should be supplemented by the sensuous ideas; in other words, by object lessons, or specimens of nature and of art in museums and art galleries; and by the work of the skilled hand directed by the trained eye of the student in workshops and laboratories. In this way the repression of original or instinctive thought by books, will be prevented.

After leaving school, the life of man, in outward action and inward thought, is guided not only by his past attainment of knowledge, but also by passing events, new discoveries and inventions; partly observed by himself, but mostly recorded in books and journals, and to a great extent in newspapers; and it is highly important for him to know in which of them to look for reliable information.

Language, as an incident of the sensuous ideas, designed to externalize, or, as it were, to express them, and thereby to communicate, record and preserve them, their combinations and results, is one of the oldest, and perhaps is the greatest and the most useful, of man's inventions. It is the most effective means of artistic as well as of scientific expression, and it should, as such, be carefully cultivated. It far excels painting and sculpture, representing not, like them, single scenes and actions; but expressing in a brief compass the whole integral action of man's spirit, his own ideas, notions, conceptions, judgments, feelings, past deeds and future purposes, and those of other persons; as in science, history, contracts, positive laws.

While, for the most part, thought disembarrassed from language, as its artificial, outward, mediate instrument, is carried on freely, and instinctively, with perfect ease and certainty, and with almost infinite rapidity, by means of its natural, inward, immediate, and original instruments, the sensuous ideas; the artistic qualities of language should be judiciously utilized. To promote the excellence of books and journals, the use of language should be taught as a fine art, and as the highest art.

But, however well written books and journals may be, still, owing to man's limited capacity for digesting them, some means should be provided to enable every person to pick out those which are suited to his needs. For this purpose, the institution of the national or international "Public Commissioners of Criticism," belonging to the complete organization of the republic of letters and art, would, when put in operation, be admirably suited.

It would pass in review, in a personal examination, or by skilled assistants, the whole body of current publications; giving in a regular periodical, shortly after their appearance, brief notices of their excellences and defects to the public; and making different short lists of old and new publications best suited, respectively, for the reading and study of persons in different situations of life.

Of course, every person would be left free to delve for himself in the general mine of letters for such hidden treasures as it may contain. But for the general public, not having the means, the time, nor the enterprise for such an investigation, the systematic action of the "Public Commissioners of Criticism" would be found a valuable aid.

It is evident, on the whole, that the irregular and unassisted use of books and other publications, must retard and contract the liberal culture that would result from persistent application of the knowledge of the First Principle of the Semitic philosophy.

90. (3) Passing now to the undue respect paid to ancestors and predecessors, as the third one of the principal difficulties before enumerated that obstruct the attainment of a universal social reformation, we have to remark, in the first place, that it participates with the

other two in the vice of retarding the free development
of the knowledge of the First Principle of the Semitic
philosophy, as the doctrine of the Kingdom of God;
and, in the second place, that it partakes of that superstitious worship of dead ancestors, which formed a part
of the ancient heathenism, practiced formerly by the
white race.

It is a very old experience that very great men often
have very great faults. In this centennial season, 1889,
commemorating the inauguration of the Constitution of
the United States, we are reminded that not only very
great men have had their faults, but also very good men;
and that while we admire the greatness and the virtues of
these men, we should neither be blind to their infirmities, nor let our veneration for their exalted qualities
seduce us into an imitation, or even an excuse, of their
errors.

True conservatism is of principle. All true conservatism must concur in developing and upholding the First
Principle of the Semitic philosophy, or doctrine of the
Kingdom of God. All true progress is the improvement,
or evolution, both of the expression, or dogmatic statement, and of the practical realization of principle.
While the First Principle, therefore, as the basis of all
true conservatism, stands fast forever, reaching unchanged back into all the past, and forward into all
future time, the expression of that principle in science
and in the fine arts, with its practical realization in
society and in the useful arts, must, as the even manifestation, or evolution, of man's inward and outward immortal life and growth, present a changing scene of eternal

progress. Hence, true conservatism and true progress are identical.

Error and crime and all unskilful work are departures from principle; and as such they are purely personal, resulting from personal ignorance and personal depravity. They are communicated and perpetuated by personal false instruction and evil example.

True social progress, as well as true-social conservatism, is a return to principle and a constant adherence to it, not only with personal repentance, but also with a due personal regard to its absolute truth and universal social application and obligation.

Experience shows that it is easier for the majority of mankind, not instructed in correct methods of thought, to follow the tradition and the examples of past generations, than independently to investigate and judge their truth and propriety. Hence results the unreasoning obsequiousness of large masses of men to the false opinions and evil examples of their forefathers. The evident remedy for this evil is the liberal culture of the masses, which would enable them to appreciate the worth and the authority of principles, and to discriminate justly the true insight and the virtues of their ancestors from their errors and their faults.

To establish, therefore, as the foundation of all instruction, the First Principle of the Semitic philosophy, or doctrine of the Kingdom of God, involving all principles, would at once stop the evil of the unquestioning reception of dogmas and practices, however long descended, inherited from the past. For whatever dogma or practice conflicts with this First Principle must be false and of evil tendency, and will be seen to be such.

91. The acknowledgment of the First Principle will clear the air in the discussion of many highly important public questions; sweeping away the misty grounds of the differences of opinion among good and able men; correcting the errors that originated in former generations, and leaving the truth of the matters in dispute clearly visible. Two of these questions, of very ancient origin, and connected with the church, will be briefly considered. They owe their importance to the new and aggressive relations of intolerance recently assumed by the hierarchy of the Roman Catholic church to the masses of the people of the United States, of all religions; and the mention of them here affords an appropriate occasion for recognizing the very different spirit of religious tolerance manifested with chivalrous daring by the early Roman Catholic colonists of Maryland, who, in striking contrast to the religious intolerance of Puritans and Cavaliers, north and south of them, only long afterwards converted to an equal spirit of tolerance, boldly proclaimed what was then a new as well as generous doctrine of religious liberty.

(a) One of these questions is involved in the public controversy now carried on regarding the expediency of religious instruction in the public schools; and one of the disputants, Cardinal Gibbons, says: "Religious knowledge is as far above human science as the soul is above the body, as Heaven is above earth, as eternity is above time." This is from the mediæval, ecclesiastical standpoint. Another of the disputants, from another

standpoint, says: "Religious truth is revealed in alle-
goric and symbolic form, and is to be appreciated, not
merely by the intellect, but by the imagination and the
heart. The analytic understanding is necessarily hostile
and skeptical in its attitude towards religious truth, and
the mingling of secular and religious instruction culti-
vates flippant and shallow reasoning on sacred themes."
[See Balt. *Sun Supplement,* July 11, 1889.]

But as it has been proved that every principle, in the
sense of a law of Nature, or a law of God, is a uniformity of the action of God, it follows that the uniformity,
or simultaneous, correlated complexity, of these uniformities, must constitute a First Principle, from which
all the special principles, both of religious and of secular
truth, or knowledge, must be deduced. Hence, religious
truth and secular truth are derived from the same First
Principle, are co-ordinate, reciprocal, and inseparable;
and they must both be taught, by the same methods of
demonstration and verification; whence it follows that
they can and ought to be taught in the same school.

It remains true, however, that society, when perfectly
organized, should assign the charge of all the schools to
a separate, appropriate and universal agency, or integral
organ, the republic of letters and art, numerically
identical and co-ordinate alike with the state and the
church, and equally independent of both; and that
while the state has temporarily volunteered, on account
of its financial resources, to support the schools, in the
absence of an efficient organization of the republic of
letters and art, it should administer them under its
general direction, as its trustee, with due regard to civil

and religious liberty, and for the equal benefit, both of a normal representative democratic state, and of a normal tolerant universal church.

92. (b) Again, the observance of this First Principle will also make clear the grounds of the still unsettled controversy about the supreme temporal government, between the hierarchy, or ecclesiastical body, on one hand, that absolutely ruled the whole mediæval Christian church, and still nominally rules the greater part of it, and on the other the modern state. The ultimate ground of this controversy, on the part of the hierarchy, is virtually the same untenable position taken by it, in opposition to the First Principle, when it claims the control of the schools. For, wrongly assuming that the religious duties of man are more important, more conducive to the welfare of the soul in this world and the next, than his secular duties, and that they are, therefore, designed to control the secular, and thus to have in an alleged superior sphere the special care and supervision of the hierarchy; while secular duties belong to the state, which is limited to them, and which must partake of their subordinate condition,—the hierarchy claims that by undertaking to regulate and enforce the religious duties, and to thereby exercise a higher function than the state, it is in dignity and in authority paramount to it, and thereby entitled to rule it. But, while the First Principle necessarily leads to the service of God by the people, in the responsible performance by them of both religious and secular duty, in the light and inspiration of civil and religious liberty, and of liberal culture, it also absolutely encourages them to freely use their own

powers of thought and of practical action, for which they are responsible, in rationally governing themselves. Hence, it as positively discountenances any self-enslavement of the people by submission to a despotic or paternal ecclesiastical government over them by the hierarchy, as any subjection of them, to any other non-representative government over them by a political despot or ring.

For, according to the First Principle, which is practical as well as speculative, the ideal, at once, of all duty and of all truth, and which is the part that God faithfully performs in the original and continuing social contract between God and man, constantly consummated without words, and designed for the help and blessing of all mankind,—man's religious duties and his secular duties, being man's part in that contract, are equally as important in their exercise as they are inseparable in their source. Every man, in consideration of God's help, which he accepts in that principle, is bound to co-operate with him by the performance alike of all religious and of all secular duties; they being demanded for helping and blessing, according to God's love and purpose, all other men.

Although to commune and take counsel with God, either alone, or while encouraging others to do the same in large or small assemblies, convened for that purpose, is the first part of man's religious duty, yet the sequel of that duty must issue, according to his means and opportunities, by the force of that principle, not only in occasional benevolent and philanthropic enterprises, but also in such a just and liberal regular conduct of his secular affairs, as will aim to promote as well the rightful interests of his fellow-men as his own. Nor will man's part in the performance of any secular duty be properly completed without religiously seeking for that purpose the aid of divine wisdom in the due contemplation of that principle, in the doctrine of the Kingdom of God.

The First Principle of the Semitic philosophy affords as little ground to the hierarchy of the mediæval Christian church for establishing non-representative ecclesiastical government over the people, or any portion of them, as for interfering with the public schools; indeed, it gives as little right to the head of that hierarchy, the Christian Pope, as to the Mohammedan "commander of the Faithful," to assert despotic "temporal power" over the people. For this principle necessarily implies the principle of the sovereignty of the people, while it imposes on the people the duty and the responsibility of maintaining a moral social order, and a normal social organization.

Yet, after the early Christian communities had each adopted as the germ and the undenominational type of modern society, or of modern civilization, the form of the association of Jesus with his Apostles, which he called the general assembly of the people, or, as it were, the town meeting, the congregation, of the people—by the Greek name " ecclesia,"—and after they had developed from the First Principle a distinctively and peculiarly Christian representative or synodal constitution, serving as a bond of unity to combine them into one Christendom, and based on the sovereignty of the people; it is a remarkable phenomenon, deserving grave consideration, and showing the seductive and demoralizing force of ancient heathen examples, that the hierarchy or clergy of the Roman church of Christendom, in the Middle Ages, by means of a separate Roman ecclesiastical government,—which ignored the First Principle of the Semitic philosophy, or Kingdom of God, and its principle of the sovereignty of the people, but was exactly modeled after the ancient heathen despotic Roman empire, and was based on the submissive degradation of the people by the power of heathen superstition and ignorance, miscalled the spiritual power,—actually succeeded in acquiring over the whole of western Christendom a supreme, despotic, and universal temporal dominion.

While, however, the pagan Roman emperors, followed in their despotic rule by so-called Christians, claimed that the right to rule and make laws was conferred upon them by a law made in regular form, the *lex regia*, by the people, (Dig. i., iv.); and they thereby admitted the original sovereignty of the people, the hierarchy does not deign to refer to the people at all as the source of its power. It asserts (Gratian's Decr. Dist. xcvi., c. x.) that "there are two things by which principally the world is governed, the sacred authority of the pontiffs, and the royal power." It also irreverently pretends that the authority and power of the pontiffs is directly granted to them as vicars or vicegerents of God; a pretense sufficiently refuted by the notoriously immoral character of more than one of those pontiffs,—a character which could not, without blasphemy, be considered as belonging to God's representative among men.

The famous simile of Gregory VII., comparing the popedom to the sun, and the temporal empire to the moon, while exhibiting his contracted ecclesiastical view in this respect, displays his want both of far prophetic vision, and of rational appreciation of the social duty imposed upon man individually and collectively by the moral force of the First Principle of the Semitic philosophy. For, blinded by the contemplation of two shining motes, as it were, of the solar system, with the larger and brighter of which he proudly identifies himself, he fails to see the boundless stellar universe of the people.

The ecclesiastical government of the Roman hierarchy is evidently a gnostic scheme of Magian or Manichean Orientalism, regarding the people as contemptible, and fit only to be deluded by Magian arts. The purely religious and the moral tenets and practices of the laity of the mediæval Christian church, and of the modern church that has succeeded it, are not here discussed or questioned. They are derived more from tradition among the laity, than from the hierarchy, which occupied itself for many generations more with government than with teaching; and then, having neglected the First Principle of the Semitic philosophy, the hierarchy fashioned its dogmas after the heathen philosophers of Greece.

But, remarkable as are the distant heathen origin and the brilliant ambitious career of the ecclesiastical government of the Roman hierarchy, still more memorable is the fact that it is dead, and has been dead more than a century, and yet is carried about unburied by the living church that it long ruled. It has succumbed gradually to successive revolutions that have developed, one after

another, the speculative and practical elements of the
First Principle; reviving thereby the original popular
tradition of the Kingdom of God, or Christianity, and
increasing the intelligence and the free instinctive thought
of the people. It has yielded, namely, to the modern
revival of letters, of science, of the fine and the industrial
arts; to the organization of industrial guilds, of free
cities, of the universities; to the representation of the
Commons in the parliaments of England, Spain and other
countries; to the Protestant reformation; to the Roman
Catholic reformation of the council of Trent; to the
English rebellion and revolution; to the American revolution, establishing, at last, the sovereignty of the people; and to the consequent French revolution, which,
whatever else it did, gave a fresh impetus to the other
revolutions by which it was preceded.

If the ecclesiastical government of the Roman hierarchy
were not now dead, it would surely put in operation the
institution which it otherwise vainly invented with fiendish malignity for the terror, and torture, and destruction
of those who actively, or in words, or in secret instinctive
thought, opposed or doubted it. But the dungeons of
the Inquisition are untenanted; its racks, its wheels, its
deftly contrived machinery for inflicting exquisite torture, are rusting from disuse; its autos-da-fe have ceased;
the smoke of its burned victims no longer ascends bearing
to just heaven the indignant protest of outraged humanity.
Its cunning and hypocritical, as well as cruel and inhu-
man inquisitors, immolating, with washed hands, their
doomed victims by the hands of the subject and subordinate civil government, for the pretended glory of God,

but really and unquestionably, to maintain, by the rule of the ecclesiastical government, the authority of the sacerdotal order,—where are they? Dead, long ago.

For Roman Catholic Italy has raised a monument in Rome to Bruno, the simple man of letters, the innocent victim whom the Inquisition malignantly burned to death at the stake, in open defiance of the right of free thought by the people, and neither has the Inquisition stirred, nor has there been proclaimed a crusade. The ecclesiastical government, therefore, with the Inquisition, must, indeed, be dead. The paper documents on which its claim to authority rested, though not repealed, as in candor they should be, are obsolete. Then peace to its ashes. This monument proves at once the downfall of the ecclesiastical government of the Roman Catholic church, and the liberty of its laity to elect their priests and bishops.

Corresponding monuments, erected by Protestants, to the victims of the ignorant fanaticism of their predecessors, would greatly tend to remove the barriers of intolerance still separating the monotheistic religious denominations.

Bruno's monument, in a generous and liberal age, must form a greater attraction for cultured pilgrims in Rome, than all its boasted heathen antiquities. An equal decoration to Geneva would be a Protestant monument to Servetus. Nor would a monument erected in New England by liberal Protestants to victims judicially sacrificed there by Protestant courts and witnesses blinded by religious fanaticism, for the impossible religious crime of witchcraft, shine in future ages with less glory than its splendid memorial of Bunker Hill.

To mark in this way, by other monuments, the departure of the present age from the errors of past generations, would serve to greatly advance the period for a general social reformation.

93. (c) Another question seeks, in regard to the general industrial war brought about by former generations, a better way; and proposes the means of a general industrial pacification. This end would be promoted by the adoption of the significant and effective popular measure, of practically inaugurating the abandonment of the ancient abuse of the interference of government in industrial affairs.

The present industrial war, aggravated by the partial interference of government in the affairs of industry, can only be composed by the independent and complete co-operative and non-belligerent organization of all the industrial classes,—the working-men, the employers, the capitalists, and the consumers. Happily, while each class is too strong to be reduced to subjection by the others combined, each is practically benefited by the prosperity of all the rest.

The class of working-men are to a great extent already organized, though not on a harmonious, liberal, and *far reaching* industrial principle; and recently, the classes of capitalists and employers, in large numbers, have jointly contrived and put in operation, with the partial assistance of the government, a system of combining their property and business, on a great scale, in special trust, for their joint benefit, in opposition not only to the class of working-men, but also to the class of consumers. But the isolated organization of the class of working-men and the joint organization of the classes of capitalists and employers, are hostile and destructive; and they mean a continuance of the present universal industrial war.

Now, a measure inaugurating the abandonment of the ancient abuse of the interference of the government in the affairs of industry, and thus promoting the harmony and co-operation of the industrial classes, by proving the capacity of the republic of industry, as an organized whole, to efficiently, liberally, and justly regulate its own interests independent of the government, would be to add to the separate organizations of the other industrial classes a general organization of the class of consumers and users, as such, of the productions of industry; but containing also bodily, in a great measure, owing to the integral nature of industry, the other ideally separated industrial classes of working-men, of employers, and of capitalists; and thereby representing the general public.

This general organization of the class of consumers would be as fully able, as it would be rationally and probably inclined, to balance and control, in strict justice and clear reason, the other industrial classes in a general system of fair wages, fair interest, fair profits, and fair prices. It would especially promote liberal and conservative competition, by discountenancing, except in the case of temporary overproduction, all unremunerative prices, and, in all cases, prices cruelly or unreasonably low; and it would thus prevent capitalists and employers from ruining each other at the expense of the working-men, and by the aid of thoughtless consumers, who would sacrifice, for a trifling present gain, not only vital interests of producers, but their own future permanent convenience.

This general organization of the class of consumers, to control the other industrial classes, and to co-operate with them, must rest on the ultimate identity of the normal or proper interests of all the industrial classes, as required and established by the First Principle, and as demonstrated by the science of industrial, as distinguished from political, economy.

94. (d) Another evil of vast importance, involving a renewal of ancient violations of Interrace law, and produced by modern legislation in the United States of America, is the body of so-called Constitutional amendments, illegally granting suffrage to the negroes. The remedy for this evil must be applied, before a general social reformation can be expected; but is embarrassed by great respect due to the strong and earnest character of the men, now departed, under whose leadership it was inflicted, in probable ignorance of its enormity, and even in the belief that it was highly meritorious. This remedy remains to be considered, with all the frankness due to its importance.

The great anti-slavery leaders, the old and staunch Abolitionists, to whose burning zeal, tenacity of purpose, energy of speech, fearlessness of action, and skilful political generalship, for liberty and humanity, the country is indebted for the abolition of slavery, have one by one passed away. Some died as martyrs; others as active partisans in the dangerous contest for their cause; and others in peace and old age, surrounded by reverent neighbors, in a halo, as it were, of local sanctity. But, so far as they were zealous and active Abolitionists in their public life, and nothing more, they deserve of their country and of the world, and they must receive, as high honors as any martyrs and saints of modern times.

It is an undeniable fact, however, that some of them went beyond the abolition of slavery, and encouraged and sanctioned, without the warrant of experience, the action of the Republican party in the granting of suffrage to the emancipated negroes. If, in this respect, therefore, the Abolitionists who did so violated a principle of the higher law, they must be treated as common men, liable to commit error and do evil, as well as to see the truth and do good. They must be content to be classed, not as immaculate saints, but as men like the worthies of the American revolution, who vindicated one principle and violated another,—asserting with immortal glory the principle of the sovereignty of the people, and violating the principle of personal liberty, by inserting in the Constitution a recognition of slavery and the slave-trade.

The abolition of the slavery of the negroes was a legal measure, neglected by the great men of the American revolution, and for which the Abolitionists, according to their share in its promotion, are entitled to all honor; because it is in conformity with the higher law derived from the First Principle, or law of God, of the Semitic philosophy. But the granting of suffrage to the negroes in the country of the white nation of America, is easily proved to be illegal, by whomsoever adopted; because it is a violation of that higher law, which, as the Interrace law, provides that each of the great races of mankind, for the preservation of its separate individuality and peculiar civilization, shall occupy a separate country.

As it is a matter of history, however, that the party of the Abolitionists were few, and were an almost insignificant ally, in point of numbers, to the Republican party, at the time of the *de facto* adoption of the measure granting suffrage to the negroes, it seems permissible to treat that measure, not only apart from all consideration of the Abolitionists, but also, notwithstanding its constitutional form, as the action, under very extraordinary circumstances, of the same Republican party which both at that time controlled the government of the United States, and is still, in 1889, after a brief overthrow, the great living political party predominant in that government. It is the Republican party, therefore, that is responsible for that measure, and which, if convinced of its illegality and unconstitutionality, must, as an honorable association, move to reconsider and repeal it.

The Interrace law is based on the old figurative proverb used by Paul, that God "hath made of one blood all nations of men for to dwell on all the face of the earth," (Acts xvii., 26); which, in connection with the other figurative saying, of at least equal antiquity, that "the blood is the life," (Gen. ix., 4, Deut. xii., 23), embodies much of ancient wisdom. This proverb is a universal proposition, expressing the fact of observation, or experience, that all men have a universal physical quality, or set of qualities, in their blood, along with spiritual qualities of equal universality. It also implies, what modern chemistry has demonstrated, that the blood of animals differs from that of man. It is a proposition that, by calling attention to a distinctive and striking sensuous idea reflected from every man, enabled early man to think distinctly of his fellow-men; to group them as a whole physically and spiritually different from animals; to compare them with each other and note their differences as well as their points of resemblance; to think of them individually as equals in the most important physical and spiritual respects, while differing in others; to think of them collectively as a nation of such men; to think of nations collectively as a race of such nations; and to think of all the races collectively as the general family of mankind.

There is also very ancient evidence, that the outward appearance, or color, of the skin, as something outwardly permanent and significant respectively, in the different races, notwithstanding both the inward oneness of blood in men, and their acknowledged general equality, was considered to mark a very great and permanent difference of character among them.   This is what Jeremiah must mean when he says: "Can the Ethiopian change his skin, or the leopard his spots? then may ye also do good that are accustomed to do evil." (Jer. xiii., 23.) The comparison, according to Hebrew usage, is double as well as elliptical. Its point is the difficulty of changing character. The Ethiopian and the leopard had fixed and unchangeable general traits of character, known to all that saw them, by the skin of the one and the spots of the other. The unchangeable skin and spots are symbolically put in the place of unchangeable character. The meaning of the prophet is that the character of him that is accustomed to do evil, is as fixed in his evil way as the proverbial general character of the Ethiopian or the leopard.

The races of mankind, thus distinguished by different colors of skin, have also been observed to dwell from immemorial time in different countries; their local separation being obviously necessary to preserve their respective individuality; and being clearly, therefore, like their individuality, of divine appointment. For Paul, in the same connection in which he says that God "hath made of one blood all nations of men for to dwell on all the face of the earth," adds immediately "and hath determined the times before appointed and the bounds of their habitation."

Hence results the Interrace law that apportions to each race of mankind a separate country, with the absolute right to its exclusive possession, occupancy, and government. Being evidently involved in the First Principle of the Semitic philosophy, the Interrace law is the paramount law of the universal society of the races of mankind.

This Interrace law was violated when the ancestors of the negro nation now in America were violently carried away, as was notoriously done, from their native country in Central Africa. For it is an unquestionable historical fact that Central Africa has been occupied from immemorial time by the negro race as its providential native country.

The same Interrace law was violated, when the negro nation, whose ancestors were thus illegally brought to

America, was permitted, by the grant of suffrage, to participate in the government of the country which was acquired by the white nation there, and to whom, according to that Interrace law, that country, with its government, exclusively belongs.

It is evident that these two infractions of the Interrace law can only be properly and efficiently remedied, and therefore must be remedied, by the return of the negro nation in America to the providential native country of their race in Central Africa.

This remedial measure, viewed deliberately, in all its magnitude, and in face of its apparently onerous aspect, as highly costly, on the part of the white nation of America, is proved, by the complicity of their ancestors, as shown by the original Constitution of the United States, not only in the enslavement, but also in the importation, and, therefore, in the forcible deportation from Africa of the ancestors of the negro nation now in America, to be for that white nation a political and legal, as well as a moral and natural, obligation.

The emancipation of the negroes has made no amends to them for the debt due them for the injury of depriving them, in their ancestors, of their native country; and as the grant of suffrage to them, in a country not their own, is illegal, it is false money, and both parties incur guilt by its use; while, if it was intended to pay the debt due to the negroes for the deprivation of their country, this debt remains unpaid with interest.

But the measure of restoring the negroes to their own original home in Central Africa, and assuring them there an ample, fertile, healthful, and independent country, by the white nation of America, has for both races, like all great measures of liberal statesmanship, affecting two distinct but rightful interests, a mutually beneficial aspect. Little need be said of its obvious material advantages to both parties. While the negro nation would acquire, by the just generosity of the white nation of America, the means of colonizing and possessing, as their own ancestral property, a country in the old land suited to their nature, with independence, and social as well as political equality, and also affording not only ample reward for all useful labor, and the energizing stimulation of establishing new and permanent homes, but also all the prizes of legitimate social, industrial, and political ambition; the white nation of America would receive, in return, the benefit of a homogeneous population, increased value of its land, and room, equivalent to new territory, for seven millions of white immigrants to take the places of the departing negroes, besides the industrial activity incidental to the movement, and to the wise expenditure it would necessitate of large sums in ship-building, commerce, manufactures, and agricultural produce.

But the chief benefit of this measure would be spiritual, or moral, religious, and intellectual; and this would consist in its efficacy to facilitate in the two races, both the present preservation and the future development of their respective modes and measures of civilization.

There is only one normal civilization, which is the knowledge and the practical realization of the First Principle of the Semitic philosophy, or doctrine of the Kingdom of God. But there are several degrees, grades, or steps of civilization attained, respectively, by the

different races of mankind, and all tending to the one
normal civilization; all capable likewise of being gradually
developed into it, and all being analogous to the shades
of culture reached by individuals.   Nations, like children, must begin civilization with its rudiments.   The
true normal civilization must be developed in the nations,
as children, by the system of exciting sensuous ideas by
object lessons, and by leading instinctive thought, with
these and other related sensuous ideas, from something
like Frœbel's Kindergarten exercises to a more or less
thorough acquaintance with, and exercise of, the First
Principle in advanced schools and universities, and in
enlightened social institutions and modes of general
social life.

The one uniform normal civilization, developed according to the First Principle, must be the ideal of civilization for all the races in their universal society.   While it
may admit of modifications in matters of indifference, it
must at least embrace, in the First Principle, the original
and continuing social contract of God with man, the
normal social organization, and the moral or higher law.

The white race, as a whole, although, owing to its general monotheistic idolatry, its prevalent vice of drunkenness, its demoralizing lotteries, and its offensive wars,
it is still very far from that ideal, has so far made, of all
the races, the nearest approach to it.   But this race is
bound to make great strides of self-improvement, before
it becomes worthy and able to convert, by its missionary
enterprises, the other races to the true standard of civilization.   It must also change its missionary methods, and,
instead of degrading the Bible by translating it into

inartificial heathenish jargons, some of which arc also vile, it should teach modern civilization, including Christianity, in one of the civilized modern languages, in every one of which a great part of it is embodied, just as the old Latin civilization was taught in Europe for centuries by means of the Latin language. Perhaps, for many reasons, and especially because it is most widely known, the best suited of the modern languages to teach modern civilization is the English.

Now, in view of the different degrees of civilization prevailing in different races, the local combination and cohabitation of two different degrees of civilization in the same country, may be rationally expected, like the joining of scholars of different degrees of proficiency in the same class in school, to be hurtful to both; checking the advance of one, and driving the other on too rapidly. In the lower, it tends, first, to promote the vices, which are easily learned, and thereby to obstruct the more difficult task of assuming the virtues, of the higher civilization; and especially is this the result where the two degrees of civilization meet in two different races, as is clearly illustrated by the disastrous contact of the white man with the red man, and the gradual extinction of the latter, in America. In the higher civilization, too, in which, even when it is isolated, vices, as survivals of an earlier degree of barbarism, may abound in some of its individuals of every class, the advent of the lower civilization, besides re-inforcing such vices, may re-introduce still more barbarous or even savage vices, which the higher has already outgrown; as was seen when the savage ancestors of the present negroes in America were forcibly brought into the white nation there, bringing with them slavery, which the whites had long ago abandoned, and which caused among the whites, for its abolition, one of the most tremendous civil wars history has recorded. Such are the effects of combining in the same country, in different races, different degrees of civilization.

He must be blind, indeed, who does not see that in measure and degree the civilization of the negroes is different from that of the white men in the United States of America. There are, it is true, a few exceptional negroes of culture and industry, who can rank in these respects with the majority of the whites; and many more of a morality and a piety as high as those of the best of the whites; and there are some exceptional whites who demean themselves as fit associates for the lowest of the negroes. But the signs of the superior civilization of the majority of the whites are unmistakably displayed wherever large numbers of whites and negroes live close together, as in the cities of the north, and in the cities and fields of the south.

Hence, as negro civilization in America is inferior to that of the whites living with them, the violation of the Interrace law by negro suffrage there, must reasonably be anticipated to strengthen the influence of the inferior negro civilization, and thereby to degrade the superior civilization of the whites, to the manifest prejudice of both races. For, since the freedom of the negroes and all the rights of person and of property which they now enjoy in America are due alone to the civilization of the whites, if that civilization should be degraded, few rights would be left to the negroes.

Moreover, the degradation of the civilization of the whites by negro suffrage, will not only affect the whites in the states where the negro population predominates, by affiliation of negroes with the whites of their own level, but in all the states. For instance, the state of Louisiana, with a large and influential negro population, has established and sanctioned, by the public authority of that state, in opposition to the civilization of the whites, a system of public lotteries, designed to gratify the immoral savage passion of gambling, which is condemned by the other states as criminal; and that public institution of the state of Louisiana, by surreptitiously circulating in other states its tickets and its illusive advertisements, in violation of their laws, is successful in daily debauching the public morals and plundering the weak and unwary in all the other states, where otherwise the civilization of the whites in this matter prevails.

The true policy, therefore, for all the states, is by constitutional amendment, or by a decision of the supreme court, or otherwise, as they may agree, to recognize and declare according to the paramount Interrace law, the illegality of the suffrage of negroes in the country of the whites.

But, when the Interrace law is obeyed, the separate and different degrees of civilization of the different races, in their respective separate countries, may all differ, and yet may all be good in their kind. For no one that observes the regular variety of things, as well as the

uniformity of laws, in the organic and inorganic worlds,
noting that no two stars, no two grains of sand, no two
leaves, no two fruits, no two animals, are exactly alike,
but that every separate thing is endowed with a special
individuality, can doubt, that, as the apple tree, the pear
tree, the orange tree, the palm tree, while all follow the
general laws and processes of vegetation, produce different fruits, all being good, and each having its different
individual excellence; so the great races of mankind, the
white, the Mongolian, the Hindoo, the negro, while all
obey their fundamental laws involved in the First Principle, will each, in time, work out, and mark with its
special individuality, a separate and distinctive, rival
degree or kind of civilization. To attain, however, their
peculiar development, the different races of mankind
must dwell in separate countries.

Civilization does not, like electricity, pass by induction from one body, collective or individual, to another;
although the marks on the sensuous ideas, the elements
of civilization, are reflected by an analogous process from
their outward objects. Civilization can only be conferred
on, or improved in, an individual or a nation by rational
and persistent educational work on one side, with earnest
co-operation on the other. Colonization, for a large body,
as the bringing up of a nation, directing and developing
its powers, and supplying its needs by another from
helpless infancy, until it is able to make its own destiny,
is evidently for both parties, the best and most stimulating educational work. For improving the inchoate
civilization already acquired by the American negroes,

their colonization in Central Africa by the white nation of America is evidently the proper means.

To facilitate the development of a true negro civilization by colonizing the American negroes in Central Africa, and to protect it there from hostile interference of the whites, the diplomacy and the Congress of the United States of America should assert the supreme authority of the Interrace law, by insisting not only that the sale of intoxicants and arms by a superior race to savages should be included in the definition of piracy, but also that Central Africa, having been immemorially the natural or providential habitat of the negro race, belongs to that race exclusively. And the United States of America should claim, by treaty with the nations of Europe, or by a constitutional amendment, the authority to protect the negro nation growing from the colony of American negroes, in its right to select, acquire and exclusively occupy and govern an ample, well located, and independent country in the central portion of Africa; not the least commendation of which establishment would be its agency in spreading light over the Dark Continent.

For this new African state, both for example and for warning, the experience of Liberia, Hayti, and San Domingo, in regard to negro civilization, should be consulted. The general legal profession, when organized, could greatly aid this enterprise by preparing for the consideration of the new African state a brief code of universal positive common law, suggested by the experience of all civilized nations, and fit for their adoption.

95. Besides the difficulties now specifically mentioned, the chief general cause of the slow, vacillating,

halting progress of the civilization of society, in all the races of mankind, is the fact that most men lack, and have always lacked, liberal culture, all-sided views; and are narrow-minded, with a contracted, one-sided outlook, being men either generally ignorant, or mere specialists, following exclusively one idea, one subordinate principle, and ignoring, or even antagonizing, all else. The removal of this one-sidedness must be the work of the liberal culture that will result from the pursuit of the one First Principle of the Semitic philosophy, in which principle all other principles are involved.

This pursuit, in which, with moderate success, the masses of mankind, by means of their sensuous ideas and their instinctive thought, aided by a public common education, can unite with the learned, will yield a unitary and universal all round view of all things; not based on the one supposed element of the ancient Greek, but on the one composed of many, the American *e pluribus unum*, the organic one, the integral one, the one of God, one universe, one humanity, one social contract, one republic of letters and art, one republic of the church, one republic of industry, one republic of charity, one republic of government, one republic of all these republics; one social order, one order of the universe.

This view will also result in one rational general conclusion of that enlightened and energized reason, which is speculative faith, from all the past and present, by analogy, to all the future,—from life to immortality, from unceasing social progress, however unsteady, to the one ultimate and perfect Kingdom of God here and hereafter, as the ideal society.

But it would be idle to expect to overthrow at once, or in a generation, or in a century, all the heathenism of the world, or of the white race, or even of its most favored nation, or most liberal church, or most orthodox. The accretions of eighteen hundred years of deleterious ancient Oriental heathenism must be stripped from the slender growth of original Christianity, before the shriveled and stunted plant can flourish, in its appointed way, like the vine of Egypt, or the tree of life.

It must be acknowledged, however, that civilization in the last few centuries, and especially Christianity, its distinguishing element, notwithstanding the counteracting influence of heathenism, has made some progress, although the road to its ultimate perfection is still a long one. The next century bids fair to make at least as great an advance of civilization among the masses, not only of the leading race, but of all the partially civilized races, in respect of philosophy, of science and of art, as well as of morality and religion, beyond the nineteenth century, as this century made over the eighteenth, and as the eighteenth made over all the centuries that went before it.

But the work to be done in the next century in furtherance of civilization, of liberal culture, and of pure Christianity, should be outlined and prepared as well as forecasted in the present. To consider well therefore, and to lay down firmly and understandingly, the plans of the coming era of social progress, in thorough public education from the lowest to the highest grades, and to provide for its sure direction a wide and certain outlook in a popular true philosophy,—is the duty of the present day.

Even the work of many future centuries of social progress can be read at this time in an embryonic form in the First Principle of the Kingdom of God, or Semitic philosophy, which, when properly appealed to, will yield all the true oracles needed for the instruction and the guidance of all coming generations.

Accordingly, its influence in the recent universal and almost silent revolution of Brazil in favor of the principle of civil representative democracy, indicates the Providential drift, as well as the irresistible power of the instinctive thought of the masses of the people, when it is properly directed by their leaders. This movement, as Canada is only nominally monarchical, virtually closes in triumph the westward march of the star of the true empire of the people; and vindicates the whole western hemisphere for the principle of civil representative democracy, with all the social reforms in Church and State which this principle necessarily involves. While, therefore, the closing decade of this century may now witness, as the sequel of this event, the consolidation and security of all the true American international interests of the western hemisphere—effected, not only by means of the present Pan-American Congress, but also by occasional future liberal international American conventions—the next century will be prepared, throughout all the borders of the Eastern Hemisphere, in Europe, Australia, and wherever else the white race dwells, among the colored races in India, China and Japan, and even in a future mighty nation of American negroes in Central Africa, to welcome the beneficent controlling power of the universal principle of civil representative democracy, as exhibited in its shining example of fraternally united free America.